# The Hole In Your Heart

*[handwritten inscription: John — Thanks for all your support & prayers. John 2-08.]*

by

## John Brownlee

xulon PRESS

# Dedication:

To the women in my life who made a significant, positive contribution to my personality formation: my mother, grandmother, and sisters.

# Acknowledgements:

I wish to express my grateful appreciation to a few key individuals who made direct contributions to encouraging and assisting me in the completing this book: Valli Van Eron, Elizabeth Regule, Jay Thatcher, Dave Sanderson, Jamie Chavez, Lori Whitbey, and Maurice Cleland. Most of all I thank my Heavenly Father, who has given me life and guided my journey of learning so I could assist others.

# Table of Contents

# Forward:  This is Me

There are three things I want to know about the author before I purchase a book.

Is he knowledgeable on the topic?

What is his motive for writing?

Does he have extensive experience in the subject?

So before you purchase or read this book I want to tell you a little about who I am and why I am writing.

The concept of *The Hole in Your Heart* evolved from my own quest into myself and from my more than thirty years as a therapist working with all types of people, ranging from violent inmates to abused children to "normal" individuals and couples.

## My Philosophy of Life

My fraternal grandmother was the most important influence in my life from childhood on. Even though she is long since deceased, I continue to feel her impact on a daily basis. Grandmother was a woman of faith, compassion, and stability. She took me to church, and to visit the sick and elderly. She demonstrated by her life how to live in faith, and be caring and compassionate. As a result of her influence, my adult life has always been focused on helping others. My personal philosophy and mission is: "Help individuals grow to reach their highest potential."

*My Early Years*

I was born shortly before World War II. During the war years, my grandparents moved into our home. Mother, Father, and Grandfather worked rotating shifts in military facilities. Grandmother cared for three small children. She made meals, packed lunches, and changed the beds for the three adult shift workers.

A few years after my grandparents moved out of the home, my father chose to leave the family and move a thousand miles away. He never returned home or communicated with us again. Mother had to work six days a week to provide for us. We three children got ourselves out of bed and off to school, and we cared for ourselves until Mother arrived home in the evening. Every Sunday, rain or shine, Mother got us up and sent us off on our six-block walk to Sunday School. These early years fostered a stoic individualism and independence in my sisters and me.

*My School Years*

"John could be a good student if he would just pay attention" was the consistent message from all my teachers. Little did the teachers know that I *was* paying attention. I was studying the teacher and the class, but not her math and science. I was always intrigued with why people behaved as they did. I developed my experiments of manipulating the teacher and the class just to watch their reaction. I hated every minute of school, except for the times I could study the human dynamics, create a little chaos, or break a rule.

In high school, I took the industrial arts program for boys who did not have college potential, only to find out I was not suited for industrial arts. The school's plan was to have us get enough credits to graduate. I barely made it. I had no career or educational plans, except get out of high school and get a job or go to the Marines.

In my junior year in high school, a young, new minister came to our church. He took a keen interest in this angry teenager without a father. How could I resist the influence of the Oldsmobile convertible-driving, basketball-playing, crew-cut preacher? How could I say no to his offer to ride with him, of course with the top down, to visit the hospitals and the sick?

Grant Layman influenced me to enter college and study for the ministry. Today I say, "I was on the dean's list the first year." Then I quietly add, "To be expelled for poor grades." At crunch time, I finally decided to see if I could do the work. I graduated with a strong grade point average. I don't know who was more surprised at this accomplishment, those who knew me or me.

## My Career

I was ordained to the ministry in 1960 and began in this field of service. After a few years, I found myself at a church three blocks from a large state university. Soon, I was enrolled in a master's degree program in counseling and sociology. Even though I had a busy church, was married with two small children, and had started a ministry to university students, somehow I completed my degree.

Bored again, and needing another challenge, I took a small struggling church in Toronto, Canada. I taught part time at the college level, cofounded a suicide and distress center, managed a youth camp, and was engaged in a variety of other activities.

I resigned from the church in 1977 and became chaplain and therapist in a maximum-security prison housing both male and female residents. This was another place to see those in emotional pain, observe human behavior, and try to bring healing. Simultaneously, I started a private practice in counseling, which I have continued over thirty-five years.

From my time working with prisoners, I began to see that most of the inmates' problems started early in their family of origin. I decided to start training social workers and foster parents who were caring for abused and neglected children to try to prevent them from ending up in prison. Also, I pursued advanced studies in Marriage and Family Therapy.

In coming to understand my pain from the hole in *my* heart, and from working with hurting people of all ages in many settings, it became clear to me that we all are carrying some hurt and pain from the emptiness in our hearts. Everyone has or will experience emotional hurt and pain that is rooted deep in the depths of their heart, even though we each believe we are immune from the hurt. It did not take long to realize there are no perfect parents, families, or children.

I write this book for you and me.

For me it is cathartic.

For you, may it help you understand the source of your emotional pain and provide you with constructive, workable actions you can take to ease the pain.

My desire is that grandmother's legacy of faith, loving, and helping will bring healing to you. And as you find comfort and healing, may you share it willingly with those about you who are in their own personal pain.

# Warning

This book will challenge you to rethink some beliefs, challenge you to think about some things you want to avoid, make you angry, and confront you with your responsibility for your life and others.

I will challenge conventional wisdom. But who ever said that conventional wisdom was correct? Millions of people smoke and don't believe the warnings about the potential of cancer but they die from cancer just the same.

I will challenge "political correctness." But since when is political correctness the truth? It is only politically correct because some powerful self-interest groups tried to make it truth and convinced the masses that they must agree or feel guilty or be shamed in public. The fact is that many things that are deemed politically correct aren't agreed to by the mass population. It is just that the public pressure is so strong that those who disagree withdraw and become silent. Or they have failed to look at the facts and can't defend their position.

It is OK to disagree with this book and debate what I say with your friends. But if you are going to disagree, get beyond your biased feelings that you probably received from your family or society. Look at the research or empirical evidence.

I have failed with this book if you agree with anything I say without evaluating the information—because then you are just taking my word in place of someone else's.

My objective is to challenge you to think and grow. My objective is to make you uncomfortable, because we rarely grow or change as long as we are content. I am not going to give you a magic cure that will heal all your pain in five minutes or less.

If you are looking for a feel-good book, don't waste your money or your time on this one. There is little personal growth value for the reader in a feel-good book. The only feel-good comes to the author when he gets his royalties.

I am not a pessimist. I am a realist who has seen more than sixty years of life and know that no one escapes without his share of pain. Some just deal with it or hide it better than others.

My mentor, the late Dr. Stan Skarsten, of Toronto, Ontario, drilled into me time and time again: "Don't be kind, be helpful." My objective is to be helpful. And although I never intend to be cruel, there are times you may think I am not very kind,—and that's OK if it makes you think. Sugar coated placebos don't bring healing. They just give a false impression that you are not ill, and that is worse than knowing the truth.

The Master Teacher, Jesus, said: "You will know the truth and the truth will set you free" (John 8:32). The word *know* used here is not intellectual acknowledgement, but to know by experience. Many years ago I saw a great poster that said: "You will know the truth and the truth will set you free." And below in fine print it said "but first it will make you miserable." Truer words were never spoken.

Here's to a little misery on your way to healing the hole in your heart.

# Chapter 1: The Hole in Your Heart

There is a hole in your heart and it is causing you emotional pain. You are not alone. Everyone has a hole in his or her heart. We are born with it. This hole keeps us from living the peaceful, contented, and fulfilling life that we believe is our entitlement. Actually, we are born emotionally empty but with the capacity to be receptive to all of life's positive experiences and emotions that will eventually fill our empty hearts.

Poets, psychologists, philosophers, songwriters, religious leaders have all historically lead the way in describing the heart as the seat of emotions. We use such expressions as "broken heart," "sad heart," "feeling like my heart was ripped out," and "stabbed in the heart." Our most popular songs are about broken hearts like "Achy Breaky Heart," "Your Cheatin' Heart." or "Cold Cold Heart." There was even the very popular and descriptive Sergeant Pepper's Lonely Hearts Club Band. We sometimes say that a person died of a broken heart, even though it's never been medically proven.

Isn't it interesting that we find it much more difficult to identify terms that describe the compassionate, loving heart? Is this possible because we are all more aware of the universal pain in the heart and its dramatic effects on us than we are of the happy feelings of the heart? Why is this? We have a universal expectation of happiness, and when the pain comes, not only does it hurt, but we have a keen sense that an injustice is being done to us we don't deserve.

## The Proposition

My proposition is that we are all born with an empty heart and we need many different people in our life to fill our heart with positive experiences and emotions. It is the emptiness or the absence of positive experiences and emotions that bring us emotional pain.

You can overcome negative experiences and emotions if you have a strong ratio of positive experiences and emotions to negative ones. As a therapist, this is quickly evident to me when I hear a client describing his pain. I often find myself thinking that the great distress is far out of proportion to the actual painful event. But when I put it into the context of the absence of many strong positive emotional experiences, I quickly see how it is the deficit of the past that is creating the pain of the present more than the reality of the present situation.

## Your Heart Has Many Chambers

Envision your heart as being composed of many sections with names on them. They are labeled "Father," "Mother," "Grandparents," "Siblings," "Peers," "Spouse," "Children," "Grandchildren," and "Significant Other Relationships."

Each person whose name is on a chamber is responsible for filling that chamber with unconditional love, acceptance, and positive experiences in order to provide us with the opportunity to be emotionally healthy. (So much for being a "self-made man.")

When we are born, each of these chambers is empty. Only the person whose name is on the chamber can fill his particular chamber. Your mother or grandmother may be the most wonderful loving person in the world but she cannot fill the void of an absent or reprobate father.

A loving grandmother or surrogate mother cannot fill the chamber that your mother has been unable to fill with positive experiences and emotional nourishment.

*The Painful Void*

It is from this void, which should have been filled in a healthy way, that the painful emotional cry comes. This is especially evident in children who act out. Their pain is so intense that they would rather be beaten for their negative behavior than ignored. They will take the abuse in the hope that somehow they will get healthy emotional food to fill the deficit in their heart chamber. The child would much rather be severely punished than ignored. He thinks, "At least now I am getting some attention, and attention may mean that they really do love me."

A young lady whose mother died when she was quite young was raised by her father; she confided that as a child she would lie in her bed and cry out to God for a loving mother. Many years later when she had a wonderful foster mother, she believed her prayers had been answered. But while the foster mother met many of the child's long desired needs, she could never fill the void of a deceased mother. However, she was contributing to filling the "Significant Other" chamber.

*A Deficiency Disease*

Dr. Abraham Maslow, in studying human motivation, addressed the question of "What makes people neurotic?" He wrote "that neurosis seemed at its core, and in its beginning to be a deficiency disease; that it was born out of being deprived of certain satisfactions which I called needs in the same sense that water and amino acids and calcium are needs, namely that their absence produces illness."[1] He further stated, "It is these needs which are essentially deficits in the organism, empty holes, so to speak, which must be filled up for health's sake, and furthermore must be filled *from without by human beings* other *than the subject.*"[2] (Emphasis Mine)

Maslow, John Bowlby and Rene Spitz, and many other acclaimed professionals have all concluded that love is a deficit need and an emptiness that has to be filled. If this love need is not met, "severe pathology results; if it is available at the right time, in the right quantities and with the proper style, then pathology is averted."[3]

*The Barricaded Door*

I have often challenged my patients to envision a large room in their hearts; from the large room there are many open doors leading to other rooms that appear to be very safe. But there is one door that is boarded and chained shut, surrounded with warning signs proclaiming, "Do Not Open." A roaring lion can be heard on the other side, and obviously the patients are too terrified to open the door. Invariably their greatest fear is behind that door.

Once I convince them they are strong enough to overcome whatever is on the other side, and they remove the boards and chains and open the door, they discover there is nothing but an old, weary, toothless, chained lion that cannot harm them. No one who had the courage to open the door ever found anything more scary or devastating than what they had feared for many years.

Many parents have had the experience of their children being terrified in the night because the child is convinced that there is a scary monster in their closet. Wise and good parents comfort the child, then help them open the door and explore the closet so they can see they are safe. This is great parenting. It teaches children that scary things need to be investigated. They need to learn that what they fear is never as scary as their imagination or bigger than their ability to cope with it.

But when parents say, "Go to sleep, there is nothing in your closet," the child lies awake with a growing fear and a life lesson: they should never investigate scary closets.

*The Fear of Self-Discovery*

One of Sigmund Freud's greatest discoveries was that the fear of knowledge of oneself is the cause of much psychological illness. We need to have the courage to explore our inner chambers and discover that where there are deficits, we can find healthy ways to supplement them while we learn to live with them.

If your mother never truly gave you the unconditional positive regard and love you expected, you *can* learn to live without the continual longing for her to fill what she is incapable of filling. You can learn to live without being angry with her, yourself, and the world for your lot in life. You can learn to live without looking to spouses, lovers, friends, medications, addictions, or destructive habits to fill the painful void.

If you objectively explore your "mommy room" and find a great deficit, you will also find that she did not intentionally withhold from you what you needed. You will find that she gave you all she had to give and possibly more than she received.

What an amazing discovery to realize that she gave you all that she had! She did not hold back. Now you can turn from being angry at her and taking it out on her, yourself, and others, to being appreciative that she gave you her all. Now you can forgive her. Give up your pain and move on. Accept your personal responsibility to find healthy ways to fill your need for your emotional nourishment and growth.

As long as you refuse to explore the caverns of your heart and see reality, you will continue imagining things are much worse than they actually are. If you refuse to explore your inner being and find healing, you will live in emotional pain, be stunted in your journey to emotional maturity, and destroy many good relationships. And your tee shirt will read, "Life is a bitch and then you die."

*When Emotional Pain Gnaws at You*

As your emotional pain gnaws at you and you refuse to face it, soon you will begin to develop negative coping mechanisms to blunt the pain. These negative coping mechanisms will destroy your chances of achieving the positive emotional response you want for yourself and from others.

Emotional pain is like living with an impacted wisdom tooth. Each day you are preoccupied with your pain and you miss the joys of life. Everything you do and every relationship you have is soured or at least looked on with a negative perspective. Opportunities for good experiences and relationships are negated.

As the pain grows, you are tempted to use stronger and stronger coping mechanisms to try to deaden the pain. Whether your painkillers of choice are pills, negative emotions, or destructive behaviors, they rule your life, deadening your feelings so you cannot even experience good feelings. Or when good things happen, you find a way to minimize or destroy them completely.

*Choosing Destructive Coping Mechanisms*

Emotionally, as the pain increases you use your coping mechanism of choice more and more—even though you know it is destructive—until you go through the functions of life dreading each day more and more.

There are innumerable destructive coping mechanisms you can choose, including anger, anxiety, blaming, self-destructive habits, food, drink, street drugs, prescription drugs, sexual addictions, fear of trying new things, depression. The list is endless.

Perhaps you've heard the old expression, "pick your poison." It is intriguing how each individual picks his own negative coping "poison." What have you chosen? You may have chosen several or changed from one to another because the first one you selected stopped working. It is typical to change from one method to another because the destructive coping mechanism only makes things worse and does not soothe the deep aching pain in the heart.

In fact, the self-destructive coping mechanism you have chosen is inflicting more pain on you than the original pain ever could. Take alcohol, for example. Typically, an alcoholic starts drinking to cover some perceived inadequacy (it usually is more perceived than real). As the body and mind become addicted, the need for alcohol becomes a much greater source of pain and loss than facing the original pain could ever have been.

Yet the original pain is still there. It is just masked by the coping mechanism—and not very well at that. As you start to deal with the alcoholism, you discover that you must deal with the original pain as well. This sequence is true for any destructive trait or habit you choose.

What poison have you chosen that you need to detoxify from?

*Worse Than Original Pain*

As you can see, there is another problem with not facing your pain. If you refuse to deal with the original pain, another experience (or the ill effectives of your destructive coping mechanisms) will inflict more pain into your life. Now your pain factor is compounded.

However, one emotional pain plus one emotional pain does not equal two. It now becomes multiples. Several separate hurts will cluster together and form a larger mass more powerful and than sum of the individual hurts.

Parents know that caring for one child and then having a second child does not equal coping with the challenges of two children. It has now compounded severalfold. One plus one only equals two in mathematical equations, but not in mental health!

The final result is that it is much less painful to extract the impacted wisdom tooth when it starts to ache than to put it off. It is best to endure a little more intense pain for a short period of time than endure growing pain that destroys every day for years. To deal with the pain, face it and "make friends with it" so you can move forward and enjoy your life.

If you discover you have a problem with your physical heart and your doctor recommends a bypass, are you going to ignore him, attempt to do it yourself or take a variety of pills to mask the pain? Or are you going to find the best surgeon, go under the knife, and feel terrible for a short period of time so you can live the remainder of your life to the fullest? Even though we are scared, we will usually do whatever it takes to keep the body alive and healthy.

Why are we so reluctant to apply the same principle to our mental health?

Sometimes, of course, even when a person is warned about the need to change his lifestyle to prevent continued deterioration of his physical health, he will choose to continue the destructive pattern. The same is true when one chooses not to pursue a healthy emotional lifestyle.

It all comes down to this question. Are you willing to change your behavior in order to live a healthier life? Or have you become so comfortable with your pain that you don't want to give it up?

## The Excitement of Discovery

Have you ever gone exploring in an underground cave? At first it is a bit scary, but soon you become enthralled with the stalagmites and stalactites.

So it is with mental health: as our fear dissipates, our excitement, wonder, and adventure increases. When we finally, reluctantly leave the cave, we can't wait to tell others what we have seen—and we can't wait to get back to the cavern. Our world suddenly expands and the thrill of adventure is with us forever.

*We are changed forever.*

Self-exploration is the same. At first it is scary, but soon we become so focused on discovery that the fear dissipates and our world expands.

## Emotional Pain is Inflicted upon Us

There are many deep emotional hurts that you did not cause and could not avoid. They have been inflicted upon you. These include being given up for adoption at birth; alcoholic parents; physically or sexually abusive parents; cold, rejecting parents; abusive siblings; an over-achieving sibling you could not measure up to; a physically or emotionally absent father; a physical or intellectual handicap; the death of a child; poverty; parental divorce—and the list goes on.

The fact is, as Scott Peck says in the opening words of his book *The Road Less Traveled*, "Life is difficult."

It is highly unlikely that you had a choice in the pain that was inflicted on you when you were young. Now you are an adult and you are endowed with the ability to think and reason and explore your own internal self—either by yourself or with the help of a professional, or both.

Now it is your choice whether you want to live in constant emotional pain and use ineffective ways to attempt to deaden the pain, or to be courageous and face it head on.

It has been said that courage is not the absence of fear—it is doing what is right even when you are afraid. If there were no fear then you would not be courageous in exploring the caverns of your heart. If there is no fear to overcome, then there is no joy in victory. Real joy and happiness only come when we have been successful over a great challenge.

Yes, there is a hole in your heart. There is a range of pain from just a little to what seems unendurable. And it is not fair that some people have more childhood pain than others. You probably did not cause your childhood pain, but you have chosen to maintain an ineffective and possibly destructive coping mechanism.

*Keeping or Overcoming the Pain—Your Choice*

Everyone has a hole in his or her heart. Some are small. Some are very large. Some have chosen to find a way to overcome their pain and others have chosen to live in or with their pain. Which are you?

Today you can choose whether or not to:

- go exploring inside your amazing heart, and see it as an exciting adventure

- face the old toothless lion behind the sealed door
- extract the impacted wisdom tooth
- choose a healthy emotional life
- live a pity party the remainder of your life
- choose drugs, alcohol or some other life destroying sedative that only makes things worse
- choose a neurotic coping mechanism
- grow into maturity or remain stunted

# Chapter 2: Emotionally Dependent

No man is an island, entire of itself; every man is a piece of the continent, a part of the main.
—John Donne, English poet, *Meditation XVII* (1572–1631)

Since each of us was born with an empty heart that is capable of emotional receptivity, we need others to start filling our insatiable cavity from the moment of our birth. It is a given that we come into this world as helpless infants in need of physical caretakers who provide us with food, clothing, shelter, protection, and guidance. Then isn't it reasonable to accept that the same caretakers must also provide us with the healthy emotional nourishment and experiences that are required to meet our mental, social, and behavioral development?

*From Dependency to Responsibility*

Since we are initially dependent on others for our physical nourishment and survival, it is reasonable to assume we are equally dependent on others for our emotional nourishment and survival.

However, there comes a time in our lives when we must begin to assume some responsibility for our physical well-being, and that increases until we are eventually fully responsible. If we are to mature into healthy adults, we must go through the evolution of moving from dependence to independence. Emotionally it is the same.

In both the physical and the emotional realms we start out fully dependent, with the expectation that we eventually become fully responsible for our lives. We are usually very insistent on taking over the physical control of our lives (just watch a two-year-old express a desire to do it himself!), but as adults we are often reluctant to take full responsibility for our emotional well-being. Maybe it is because we need to keep someone around who we can blame for our struggles and failures.

*No Man is an Island*

Thomas Merton, an acclaimed Catholic writer, social activist, and monk, chose this title for one of his books, making reference to John Donne's famous poem. Merton's premise is that we are part of the greater world community and must give and receive if we are to fully discover ourselves. He wrote:

> What every man looks for in his life is his own salvation and the salvation of the men he lives with. By salvation I mean first of all the discovery of who he himself really is. Then I mean something of the fulfillment of his own God given powers, in the love of others and of God. I mean also the discovery that *he cannot find himself in himself alone, but that he must find himself in and through others* (emphasis

mine)... It is contained in another saying from St. Paul: "We are all members one of another."[4]

Merton was discussing how dependency needs to evolve into interdependency. It is not about starting out life being independent and not needing anyone and remaining selfish all one's life or not giving to others. It is about ultimately seeking to become interdependent and focusing on that throughout your life. It is about receiving from others so that you can become a contributor to others and forge interdependency. Albert Einstein said it this way: "A person starts to live when he can live outside himself."

*Death by Deprivation*

Throughout most of the mid-twentieth century, Dr. René Spitz, a brilliant psychoanalyst, devoted himself to studying the relationship between a mother and her child. Over fifty years ago he studied the extremely high infant death rate in an undisclosed country. In studying an orphanage, he discovered that the children were very well cared for, yet they continued to waste away and die, rather than thrive. He concluded that death was due to a lack of physical touching and nurturing. He used the term *morasmus* to describe their condition.[5]

Dr. Spitz confirmed once and for all that human beings are born with both biological and emotional needs. He and many others have clearly shown that it is critical that every child, from birth, needs to form strong positive emotional attachments to a primary caretaker, preferably the mother, in order to thrive physically and emotionally. When infants are not touched or cuddled lovingly, they experience stress and anxiety. When touch is harsh or hurtful, an infant may believe that his natural needs are dangerous. Many children have been observed in third world countries rocking back and forth and attempting to hold and comfort themselves. Several years ago when communism fell in Romania and the country was opened up for the world to see on television we saw this tragic deprivation among the babies. It is not even debatable that touching and emotional nurturing is essential to developing healthy attachment. It is not optional!

We are not isolates who somehow grow up without being developed and influenced by the significant others around us. We are born with very sensitive receptors to all the emotional stimuli in our environment. Infants are considerably more sensitive to the emotions around them than we adults. As we age we desensitize our emotional sensors and the awareness of our environment.

## *Your First Decisions*

In our first few months of life, we are intellectually awake and begin to make decisions about ourselves, others, and the world around us.

If, as infants, we are left in filthy smelly rooms, with dirty diapers, hungry from neglect, or we are handled roughly, we will most likely conclude that the world stinks and the people in it are very uncaring. On the other hand, if our caretakers are caring and sensitive to our needs, we will most likely form a more positive view of the world.

The obvious conclusion is that we need others to fill the empty chambers in our heart. And there is good news: if we do not get adequate nurturing as children, there is a second chance for us as adults. We can learn to nurture ourselves! Ironically, the best adult self-nurturing we can do is to nurture others. For it is in genuine giving that we receive.

I have many years of experience in observing hundreds of very young children taken from abusive and neglectful homes and placed in caring foster homes. From this experience, I can only conclude that the children have already formed their first worldview. Foster parents are often disappointed when they cannot quickly and easily change the perspective and behavior of young children with their loving care. They are shocked to discover how seriously emotionally damaged the children are and how reluctant they are to trust and respond to love. I have seen many very small children who were so emotionally deprived that it was clear they had concluded that they would never respond to love and compassion, even after many years in a nurturing foster home.

I recall a six-year-old girl who was horrifically physically and sexually abused who had developed multiple personalities as a way to escape her pain. She, like thousands of others who were deprived and abused, shut down her normal emotional sensors and responders and retreated into her inner world.

One day a very loving foster parent couple sought my opinion about them adopting the four-year-old foster girl they had in their home. I responded by saying there is no way to predict how she would choose to deal with her deprivation and pain as she reached her adolescent, teen, and adult years. They chose to adopt the little girl with the understanding and commitment that they would do all in their power to give her a real chance at becoming all of which she is capable.

I have seen adopted children in some of the most caring, giving homes you can imagine reject it all and literally put their parents and siblings through hell. Tragically, they had formed a very negative view of life from their first moments on earth and not even the finest of families could help them develop a healthy emotional bond or maturity. These are extreme cases but represent how people may respond to their emotional pain out of their empty father and mother chambers.

*Prenatal Influence*

We are not born with our hearts and minds imprinted with a perspective on life, values, emotions, or feelings. We are not birds that are imprinted with a specfic set of activities necessary to live. We are human beings, created to begin learning from the moment of birth.

And now there is considerable evidence that our perspective on life is formed in the prenatal stage. Dr. Thomas Verney, a world leader in prenatal studies, has a written a great book, *The Secret Life of the Unborn Child,* in which he clearly describes how the unborn infant responds to various external stimuli and how that impacts the child.

# Chapter 3: It Takes A Healthy Family

Remember that our hearts have many empty chambers (figuratively speaking, of course), and each chamber can only be filled by the person whose name is on the chamber. *No one can fulfill someone else's chamber.* The hole in your heart is either filled in a healthy, positive, nurturing way by that specific person, or it is corrupted or only partially filled.

*The Mother Compartment*

Obviously, mother is the first person the child has contact with, beginning with the prenatal state. Dr. Verney has shown that if a mother smokes, the cigarette smoke agitates the unborn infant. When certain types of harsh music are played, the infant shows agitation. (Interestingly, prenatal babies don't like Brahms' Lullaby. They much prefer the soothing sounds of Vivaldi.) Research clearly indicates mothers who read to their prenatal children produce children with higher intelligence. It is clearly known that mothers who are drug addicts can deliver drug-addicted babies. Obviously, if a mother can negatively influence her child in the prenatal stage, she can also positively influence her infant.

As the child enters the world, it is essential that the birth mother communicates warmth, caring, love, and acceptance. Mothers need to convey a positive emotional well-being in order to fill the mother hole in the child's heart. As the child grows into adolescence, he must be continuously fed and nurtured.

There can be good mother surrogates who care for the child and teach the child life skills. But they are not *mother*. Every child needs a special bonding with his mother that comes through their emotional contact and activities together.

Listen to another adult talk about how they learned something or spent special time with their mother—compared to talking about an experience learned from a mother surrogate. Any adult can sit and listen to a young child read. But there is a special pleasure for the child in learning to read from a loving mother.

There are many wonderful adoptive mothers and foster mothers who dearly love and nurture their chosen child. Many of these children will turn out to be healthy individuals and give praise to the mother who chose them. However, deep in the recesses of their hearts they are aware that something is missing, or they block out the thoughts and feelings to avoid the pain. They wonder why they were given up, regardless of the explanation given. Not only do they miss many things about knowing who they are, they also wonder about their ancestral history. These children grow up with emptiness in their mother and grandparent chambers that no one else can fill.

If the birth mother is good at providing the essentials of life, but lacks the ability to give emotional food to fill the hole in the heart, the child will also grow up with a deficiency in that chamber that can never be filled. If a mother dies or abandons the child, no one can ever fill her role. Most likely the child will grow up with a hole in his heart that will be very painful.

As that child grows up, he will try to find some way to satiate the pain. The coping mechanism he chooses can either be socially healthy—like working hard to build excellent relationships—or self-destructive, like withdrawing, retreating, shutting down emotionally, or acting out negatively.

We must dispel the myth that all mothers are somehow innately nurturing. They, like all of us, are born with the potential to nurture, but if they themselves have not been loved, how will they know how to automatically give it to their children? The fact is that some mothers are good at caring for the physical needs of their children but seriously lack the ability to provide emotional nurturing. If you doubt this, take a look at several different mothers and see how differently they express affection to their children and other adults.

Like several other countries, Germany has "baby-drops"—hatches in hospitals where mothers can anonymously deposit their newborns rather than killing them.[6] In the first three months of 2007 over twenty-three babies, in Germany, were killed by their mothers because they did not want them. So much for the theory that mother's have a natural instinct to protect and preserve her baby!

We easily accept that mothers must learn how to feed, diaper, and care for the physical needs of their child. They either learned this as children from their primary caregiver or they choose to learn the skill as an adult. The same learning method applies to the emotional nurturing. Some mothers have never been the recipients of good nurturing. Some mothers have chosen to work hard and invest the time and energy into learning how to give their child what they themselves did not receive.

Just as mothers can provide healthy parenting to their children, they can also teach their children very destructive ways. Words and behavior can teach children how to be deceitful, dishonest, and selfish, traits that will likely follow them into their adult lives. It's possible they will then pass this knowledge on to their children.

*The sins of the parents will be visited on to the children to the second and third generations.* This nugget of truth can be found several times in the Old Testament of the Bible. It means the parent's negative behavior will be repeated in future generations; it does not mean the children are predestined to such behavior. That is, what we are exposed to in our early developmental stages we are *likely* (but not predestined) to repeat. Even if we hated how our parents treated us. The more you protest about not being like your father or mother the more likely you are more like them than you want to admit. Take a good look. Or is it too painful?

Many of you are very angry with your parent(s) or grandparents because you believe they should have loved you completely and given you unconditional love. Your anger comes from a false premise. Do you really believe they had more to give you but chose to withhold it from you?

Personally speaking, I have rarely seen a parent intentionally and consciously withhold emotional nourishment from her child. Maybe it is time for you to accept the fact that your parent(s) gave you all they had received and possibly even more than they were given. If you want to understand your mother's coldness or harshness, take a look at who parented her. The purpose of examining your family is not to condemn, but to understand. The goal is not to blame, but to learn.

My advice for mothers would be this: if you did not receive what you wanted and needed from your mother, you need to make a conscious effort to learn how to love and nurture your child. Do you give unconditional love to your children? Hug them? Tell them you love them? Tuck them into bed at night and sit, read, and listen to them? Say a prayer with them? Or do you send them to bed alone? Don't pass on your family deficiencies just because it was the way you were parented—even if you think you turned out all right. You can chose to give your children more than you received.

*The Father Compartment*

The father's role in the emotional development of either the male or female child is just as critical as the mother's. All too often in our society we discount the importance of fathers. And all too often the father is either physically or emotionally absent. In either case, he leaves a great void in the child's life when he is absent. To put it simply, male children need a role model who shows kindness and love along with strength and disciple. The female child needs the same combination of love and firmness to affirm her sexuality, self-esteem, and identity.

I have a hole in my heart that can never be filled. The morning my mother started into the first signs of labor indicating I would be born later that day, my father chose to go squirrel hunting. In my early childhood my father was emotionally—and often physically—absent, even though we lived in the same house. In my adolescence, he deserted completely and I did not see him again until my late teens. I never had a father who tucked me in, read me a story, played ball, took me fishing or taught me how to be a good father or husband. This father cavity in me is very empty. As an adolescent and teen I was very angry and acted out in many inappropriate ways. In my adult years, I came to accept the reality of the emptiness.

Acceptance has brought healing to the hole in my heart. Understanding, forgiveness, and focusing on my positive blessings has dulled the pain. It is out of this awareness of the emptiness of my father chamber that I have developed these concepts I am sharing with you. I know about emptiness. This is not an abstract theory.

When my daughter was born I did not know the first thing about physically caring for her. I wanted to participate in her care so I soon learned the diapering and feeding procedures. As she grew she taught me how to play with Barbie dolls. Providing her with emotional nurturing came easy because I wanted to give her the very best of life and fulfill my father role of meeting her needs. Caring for her physical and emotional needs was a choice and a responsibility I took seriously.

Fathers often have greater difficulty caring for the physical or emotional needs of sons, especially if they did not have it modeled for them. Therefore, it is critical that fathers make a conscious decision to learn to be a nurturing dad who gives special time to his children, particularly if they have not experienced a good father-son relationship.

As sons or daughters grow into childhood, a father should try not to deny his children what they need from a father relationship just because he doesn't know how. He should take as much interest in learning how to be a great dad as he does in learning mechanical, technical, or business skills. It never ceases to amaze me that a father would choose to remain ignorant in knowing what his son or daughter needs, yet quote sports scores that are twenty years old or discuss the merits of what fishing lures to use. Who cares what the sports score was if you fail to give priority to raising and nurturing your children? It is a sorry state when fathers spend hours on the golf course on Saturday and very few minutes with their children; someday those fathers will be golfing alone and wondering why their children don't call or come to see them.

If it is difficult for you to be a father to your children because it was not modeled for you, you must choose to learn. If you don't know what to do, don't be ashamed to ask for help or possibly read a parenting book instead of a sports magazine. Another way to learn is to observe what other fathers are doing with their children. I guarantee your children are going to get your time; the only choice you have is whether it is good time or bad time. Children will get your money too; you can choose whether it will be money spent building good memories... or on lawyers. There is no TV program or other activity that is more important than spending time with your children.

If your father chamber is empty, there is nothing natural about parenting your son or daughter. However, as long as you have a brain and a heart you are capable of learning to give what you did not get. The fathers I greatly admired are not so much those who do it naturally, because of what they received. It is the fathers, who work hard to learn how to give out of his emptiness.

If you think having, an emotionally present father is not important take a look at the terrible violence inflicted on families and society by male and female teens and adults who lacked healthy father role models. It is common to see the depravity of attitude and skills he displays as a husband and father. Look into their hearts and you will often see the empty father chamber.

Look behind the scenes of the destructive behavior of most people and you will usually find some level of emotional deprivation.

You must learn how to live with your deficiency, just as you would have to learn how to live with a physical disability.

When I worked in a maximum security prison that housed both males and females, I noticed that the common element in the majority of cases was an emotionally or physically absent father. This was even more significant than an emotionally or physically absent mother. The most recent research is revealing over seventy percent of all males in prison had little or no contact with their birth father. This is not to suggest that these adults should be excused for their behavior. It is all too common in our society for a destructive person to play the victim role as an excuse for their behavior. Once we become adults, we are responsible for our behavior regardless of our pain, yet many people will spend more time trying to find out why their car won't run than examining their internal dysfunction. There are many good citizens in our society who have experienced the same deprivation and intense emotional pain, yet they have chosen to overcome their emptiness so they can contribute to their family and society in a positive way.

There is an appalling rate of physical and sexual abuse of their children by fathers and stepfathers, because fathers didn't have proper fathering models to follow, possibly because they were abused themselves. Often, fathers, out of their deprivation, pass their pain on to their children. Much of the abused daughter's pain comes from the father's inability to properly love her. If father or step-father had fulfilled his role in providing healthy emotional food for her heart, there would not be any sexual abuse that caused her great pain. Many deprived fathers have acted in a depraved way. Many others have chosen to not pass on the family depravity.

Let me say again: there is no excuse for passing on depravity just because it was part of your past. Be an adult, deal with your pain, and don't pass it on to your children and grandchildren.

If your father did not fill the father hole in your heart no one else can, regardless of how much they care for you. You must learn how to live with your deficiency, just as you would have to learn how to live with a physical disability.

If you are a father who is separated or divorced from the mother of your children, don't punish the children because of your anger toward their mother. Grow up. Get over the anger. Don't divorce your children. They need you. Research indicates that fifty percent of all children in single parent families saw their father three or fewer times in the previous year. This is frightening. We are creating a generation of children who have great emptiness and pain in their father chamber.

So if you are a father, start today to learn how to give the best to your children so they will not act out in destructive ways or otherwise live unhappy lives. "Your children are not your hobby; they are your calling."[7] You can stop the pattern of pain right now.

## The Grandparent Compartment

I am a firm believer that wonderful nurturing grandparents are essential to the total development of a healthy heart. I am not talking about the doting grandparent who allows the child to be unruly, selfish, or a "brat." This is not healthy. Excellent grandparents provide a balance of love and discipline.

Spoiled children are not children who are loved too much. They are children who are not properly disciplined. Unruly children are unloved. There is no such thing as giving a child too much love. When you genuinely love children, you properly discipline them so they can grow into likeable, mature, successful, responsible teens and adults. Spoiled children who become narcissist adults are lonely people.

Grandparents can provide a type of acceptance and nurturing that is quite different from what the parents provide. The child believes his parents are supposed to love and care for him. When caring and love comes from a grandparent, that is extra and unexpected, so grandparents can be the first people in the child's life who gives him unconditional positive regard that he does not expect. Empirical evidence very strongly suggests there is a significant emotional difference between adults who had a strong positive influence from a grandparent or grandparents and those who were deprived of a loving grandparent relationship. Ask your friends about their relationship with their grandparents and watch those who had great relations "light up" and enter a deeper emotional zone level.

Today, as the American family disintegrates by divorce, conflict, or distance, one of the tragic results of this trend is that many children do not have access to the blessings that good grandparenting can provide.

My professional experience has shown that where there is the absence of consistent positive grandparent influence, there is a much higher possibility of anger, violence, or addictions. When the family disintegrates, children and teens often turn to the "street corner gang" to be their source of wisdom, support, identity, and belonging. Once this happens, kids are headed for trouble.

There is something quite intriguing in how children who have a good relationship with an adult other than their parents will still accept guidance and correction more easily from the grandparents or extended family members than their parents. This applies to established relationships with other significant adults whom they have come to respect, as well.

During the second World War, when I was a preschooler, my grandparents lived with us and my grandmother cared for us so our mother could be "Rosie the Riveter." This was invaluable in my life formation. Mother gave my sisters and I many good attributes, but my grandmother gave us others. My sisters and I were doubly enriched from the maternal side, even though the fraternal side is nothing to brag about.

Instead of being jealous of the positive relationship between their children and their parents, parents should support and encourage it. This allows the grandparents to fulfill their responsibility by filling the grandparent chamber in their grandchildren's hearts. Remember, you cannot be everything to your children! They need much more than you alone can give.

Grandparents should take an active role in your grandchildren's lives so you can fill the grandparent cavity in your descendant's life. Even if your child has divorced and your grandchildren are living with the other parent, do not desert them. One of the great tragedies of divorce is not just that a child loses considerable contact with one parent, but that he often loses an entire extended family that loves him.

*The Sibling Compartment*

Parents and grandparents can teach you much about life. But siblings have an important place in helping you become a more complete person. It is amazing what siblings can teach each other about life and relationships. For example, it is much easier for the married man to understand his wife if he had a sister or sisters. Siblings can learn about teamwork, sharing, caring, fighting, and negotiating. And when someone says he had a much older sibling, but never really got to know him because of the age difference, you will quickly see the emptiness of the sibling chamber being expressed as regret and loneliness.

In assisting an executive client with his career exploration, I noticed he was an exceptionally caring executive, husband, and father. I came to learn that he had a younger sister who was born severely mentally handicapped and he was the sibling who gave her considerable special attention, even far beyond what his father did. As our discussion progressed, he realized for the first time that his handicapped sister had formed an important part of who he was. He soon made another trip to visit his now institutionalized sister, even though he knew she would not know him.

If you did not have siblings to fight with, or do mischievous things with (or to), you missed out on an important part of your childhood and adolescent development. Fighting and doing mischievous things with other kids is just not quite the same because soon you each go your separate ways and you are left alone with your memories. When your parents pass on you must go into the future alone, without other family members with whom to identify and discuss family memories.

Tragically, sometimes parents allow siblings to be abusive to each other. I vividly recall a tragic situation where for many years an older sibling would frequently scream at the younger brother, "You are an illegitimate bastard and I wished you had died the day you were born." Unfortunately the parents were too weak to stop this and you can imagine what it did to the boy's self-esteem. And guess what he became? He became a garbage collector. Being a garbage collector is a noble career; however, it was not a coincidence after years of verbal abuse.

The primary sign of a healthy sibling subsystem is when the children can celebrate each other's accomplishments, when they can rejoice in each another's successes and victories without put-downs or otherwise demeaning the accomplishment.

Life was tough squeezed between an honor roll sister two years older and one eighteen months younger who was sometimes taller than me. Yes, there were times I would have happily sold them both (cheaply). It has taken some time, but today I am grateful for all they taught me—and that I don't march into the future without family. And besides I know I am mother's favorite.

*The Spouse Compartment*

Marriage is a great mystery and a conundrum. Who can understand it? Why would anyone in his right mind sign up after looking at it logically? Just ask any ten-year-old boy what he thinks of girls and marriage. However, at some point our eyes connect with someone and God plays a little trick on us, instantly releasing the oxytocin hormone in our brain that makes it impossible for us to be logical and walk away. (Oxytocin is also released when we are being sexually intimate, which contributes to couple bonding.) I call this *euphoric psychosis*. We are in a state of euphoria and totally out of our minds. When the male is in this state he even allows his girlfriend to drive his new car—and if she wrecks it, he is only concerned about her. When the euphoria wears off and the same thing happens, his words and tone will be very different.

Even after you go through a very painful marriage and divorce and vow never to marry again, you are always at risk of the hormone getting released again. You find yourself at the altar saying out loud "I do" and wondering inside, "How did I get here?"

The old adage is men marry for sex and women for relationships. This is not far from the truth but let's not deny the woman's sexual desire as well. She just tends to be a bit more discreet. Nor should we deny that a man needs and wants a relationship more than he is likely to admit.

Some family theorists teach that we marry in order to complete ourselves. There is much truth in this. It is amazing what husbands and wives try to teach each other about themselves, life, and relationships. Yet each one finds it very difficult to listen to the other. When I see a couple going through a marital crisis I usually wonder (and sometimes come to know) why they need this. They *need* this struggle to help them complete another part of themselves or to have a second chance to get a previous experience right, one that did not turn out well the first time.

If we listen carefully to the great psychologist Alfred Adler, we would hear him say, "All behavior has a purpose" — even if the behavior is very painful or appears to be self-destructive. There is a purpose in our marriages even if they are painful. The question is, will you learn the lesson before it is too late or are you determined to go through the same pain again and again?

The truth is we *do* need another close to us to help us on our journey toward self-knowledge and self-improvement. We can never know ourselves by only looking at ourselves. This will only give us a distorted image, like walking through the carnival tent of mirrors. It is in interaction with others that we come to know ourselves and have the opportunity to grow. Of course, some choose to never learn and are doomed to repeating the same mistakes and enduring the same pain multiple times. Insanity, it's said, is doing the same thing over and over again while expecting different results.

The problem is not with the commitment of marriage. The problem is that many go into it consciously or unconsciously with the wrong expectations. For example, a woman enters a relationship with a man to help her fill the deficiency in her father compartment, then she is frustrated when her husband cannot fill the void she brings into the relationship. Or the man brings in the expectation that somehow this woman will meet his need for nurturing that he did not get from his mother. In either case, the situation is headed for trouble. Most individuals who did not get their parenting needs met express that they are not going to marry someone like the parent(s) who frustrated or hurt them, yet many do it not only once but sometimes repeatedly.

Additionally, they have a child with the expectation that the child will fill that desperate desire for love and nurturing only to be frustrated again because the baby cannot fill the emptiness in their father or mother hole in their heart. It is so tragic to see, usually a mother, try so desperately to get from their child the love and acceptance they never received as a child themselves. The anger and rage becomes even greater when their parents who deprived them gives their child what they always wanted. The anger increases because now they are thinking "all along my parents withheld from me what they could have given me." Even though this is an incorrect conclusion, they are unable to see the truth. This scenario frequently strengthens their sense of inadequacy and the belief they are loveable. This becomes a great precursor for depression and sometimes the baby becomes the target of their anger and is abused, neglected and sometimes killed.

Marriage is the opportunity for two adults to fill their spousal compartments in their journey to self-improvement. It is in giving altruistically that we move another step forward on our journey. We cannot reach self-actualization if we only stay in love with ourselves and never reach outside ourselves. Albert Einstein said, "A person starts to live when he can live outside himself." Unhealthy self-love is actually selfishness and is the road to narcissism.

The four foundation stones essential to a healthy marital relationship are companionship, sharing, affection, and sex. Companionship is what you do together. This is about playing together and having common experiences. Couples need to have things in common so they can become each other's best friend. Sharing is about sharing your hopes, dreams, worries, and fears and becoming vulnerable to each other by opening up your heart. Sharing is not about talking about Billy's need for new running shoes or Suzie's ballet lessons. Affection is affection for affection sake, not affection that is a prelude to sex. A man should learn how to hug and show affection to his companion without contemplating how quickly he can get her into bed. When men live with the perpetual image and agenda of sex in their minds, women begin to draw away from any affection at all—and then are accused of being cold. This behavior is a common source of marital conflict that all too often ends in affairs or divorce.

The spouse compartment needs to be filled with altruistic mutual nurturing and acceptance or soon the deficiency will turn to pain. The pain will soon come out in innumerable and disguised ways in the relationship.

When I watch a candle lighting ceremony at a wedding I frequently want to stand up and protest. You know the scene: two lit candles representing the couple and a big unlit candle in the middle. The bride and groom light the middle one and then blow out their own candle. No! No! No! Light the middle one as a symbol of the new relationship but don't extinguish your own life. Keep your individuality! This is what attracted you to each other. Keep your uniqueness! This is what makes you interesting. In many long-time marriages one cannot tell the man from the woman. They blend into each other so much that they and their marriage are bland and unexciting. Others might see this and admire their oneness, but is this oneness, or an unhealthy symbiotic relationship? When one dies, so does the other.

Many years ago I observed an extreme example of this when an elderly man died and his wife of over sixty years kept saying, "They are not going to bury him without me." Everyone just dismissed the words of the grieving widow, but on the morning of her husband's funeral she willed herself to her death. (This was not an act of self-harm.) The funeral was delayed and they were buried together a couple days later. This is a classic case of a symbiotic relationship where one was incapable of living without the other. If your loved one dies or abandons you it is appropriate to grieve, but it is inappropriate to die. Like the cycle of nature, you may go dormant with grief, but reemerge later with a new life.

## The Children Compartment

Why would anyone in his or her right mind want to have children? They are obnoxious, keep you up at night, demand you spend your money on them, take the time you wanted for yourselves, and one way or another, break your heart and bring you intense pain. But we have this compartment inside us labeled "Children" that cries out to have children to fill this void. God plays another one of His tricks on us and releases a hormone in our brain so that we just can't resist having children.

From the moment of conception, our children change us and our lives in ways we could have never dreamed. (Those of us who are observant parents stand back, watch and chuckle because we know what is coming.) Your child's entrance into this world will come as complete shock to your system even though you had nine months to prepare. When we touch them for the first time, we are changed forever. We will never be the same again.

My children were born in the dark ages: fathers were sentenced to the "Fathers Waiting Room" and tortured with old movies. Even if a father wanted to participate he was not permitted (and the community wondered why the father was not more bonded to his children). After three days of looking at my daughter through a glass window I finally got to touch her when we arrived home. I shall never forget the shiver that went to the depths of my soul. It opened the door of my children compartment and changed me forever. I believe thousands of fathers might tell a similar story.

Dr. Nathan Ackerman, the father of family therapy, said it best: "We raise our children and our children raise us." Reflect on what your children have taught you and how you have become a better and more self-fulfilled person. Children will find the vulnerable spots you thought you had hidden so well that no one would ever discover them.

Our society is experiencing a new phenomenon as a great number of single women, resigned to not marrying or giving birth, are turning to adoption to fill the empty children chamber. This can be very fulfilling for both mother and child so long as the mother does not seek to have the child fill *all* her empty heart chambers. This is, as we have seen, impossible. The result will likely be an unhealthy symbiotic relationship where the child can never escape the strangle hold.

It is appropriate to allow your children to fill the children compartment in your heart. But you will get into big trouble if you expect children to fill the deficient "Father," "Mother" or "Spouse" compartment. You should never have children with the expectation that they are going to take away the emptiness of the other sections of your heart. Let children be children and don't expect them to be surrogate parents.

*The Grandchildren Compartment*

Grandparents can be so obnoxious when talking about their grandchildren. So if you are not a grandparent do not get annoyed, bored, disgusted and angry when a grandmother pulls out her portfolio of seven thousand pictures and begins the bragging. I just have one suggestion for you: don't judge too harshly until you have a grandchild to fill your grandchildren compartment that has been empty since your birth. Now you can live on into the next generation through them, even though you will eventually die.

I have had the pleasure of feeling the shock that went into the depths of my soul when I held my two grandsons, who were only three months apart in age, one in each arm. My grandchildren chamber opened wide and out came the rush of emotion as the tears streamed down my cheeks. (See, I am as obnoxious about bragging about my grandchildren as anyone. I just could not resist. Let's blame it on my grandchildren compartment that needs to be filled, or on some biological dysfunction beyond my control.)

The old adage is true: if I had known that grandchildren were going to bring me this much happiness I would have skipped the children and gone directly to grandchildren!

*The Significant Others Chamber*

The last, but not unimportant, chamber is labeled "Significant Others." This is the chamber in which all the other good persons in your life have added to your emotional enrichment. Significant others are aunts and uncles; cousins; school teachers; neighbors; religious teachers and leaders; the non-family members you called "aunt" or "uncle"; childhood, teen, and adult peers; your friends' parents; step-parents; counselors; and the innumerable and often forgotten persons of all ages and walks of life who were a positive influence. Sometimes they were in your life for many years and other times they only passed through, but they left their mark on you.

Many times these were the people who kept you believing in yourself, encouraged you. Sometimes they were the only reason you chose to live rather than take your own life. These individuals gave you time and taught you skills. They listened to you describe your hurts and pain—or they just knew that you were in emotional pain even though you did not tell them. You knew they knew and cared.

For some of you this is the most fulfilled chamber in your heart. It is out of this chamber that you found (and still find) the energy and determination to go on. It is out of this chamber that you find that you were loved. You were accepted unconditionally, respected, and encouraged to go forward to be all you can be. While these significant people could not fill the other holes in your heart, somehow they gave you the strength and joy that was essential for you to carry on.

Adult peers is one last group that we need to include in the Significant Other chamber in your heart. It is essential that you as a single or a couple build a group of positive, supportive peers around you. These are friends who are always ready and willing to help you, as you are to help them. These are singles or couples that you can share time with alone or with your children and family and their children and family.

Since most parents are concerned with their children's peer group, here is a great way for you to pick your children's peers. Select a few families that you have something in common with who have children the same age as yours. Frequently plan family outings or game nights in each other's homes. This is a time for your children to learn to relate to other adults and for them to develop a peer group that you have selected.

Finally, I want to challenge you to take time to start writing a journal about all of the Significant Others who have blessed you. This needs to be a journal you add to for the remainder of your life. Over time, more and more people and events will come to mind. You will be amazed at the length and diversity of the list. You might even consider writing thank-you notes to these people!

Now, also, it is time for you to become a Significant Other. It is your turn to listen to hurting kids, or just be there. It is your turn to make your home a place of refuge for children who don't want to go home. It is your turn to be an encourager. It is your turn to take a child or teen to church with you. It is your turn to make a significant contribution to someone else's Significant Other chamber.

*It Takes a Healthy Family*

It takes a family to raise a healthy child and a healthy family to prepare the child for the challenges of the community. If each person accepts his responsibility to fill the emptiness of those he is responsible for, we will raise emotionally healthy and whole individuals who in turn will develop a healthy society. No society has ever been healthy enough to create and nurture healthy families. This is one of the tragedies of our society today: families are giving up their responsibility to raise their children to the school and the community—and then wondering why their children are so dysfunctional. Since parents have surrendered their responsibility to the school and community, there has been an exponential rise in depression, emotional illness, crime, violence, suicide, teen pregnancy, and a poverty of values.

May I challenge you to do your part as a mother, father, grandparent, sibling or other significant person in a child's life to take your role seriously? Understand that you are the only one who can fill certain emotional needs in a child. You would not deprive the child of food and watch him die from malnutrition would you? So why deprive them of food for the heart and soul?

Leo Tolstoy wrote, "All happy families resemble one another; each unhappy family is unhappy in its own fashion." To see the list of the traits of a healthy family see Appendix A.

By now you are probably asking some critical questions like:

- What if my parents or other family members did not fill my empty chamber?
- What if I don't get married, have children or grandchildren? Are you saying I am deficient?

- What can I do to become more emotionally healthy and erase the pain from the holes in my heart?
- What are the symptoms of an empty heart?
- Is there hope or must I continue to live with this pain?
- Can the good one person gives me fill the emptiness of another section of my heart?
- What happens if someone who loved me dies, will my compartment be empty and bring me pain?

These are critical questions and we will answer them in the following chapters. Don't despair. There is hope. Many people have gone before you who have had less than positive experiences. Many have learned how to deal with their pain and met their own needs.

Don't quit now. Keep on. There are lessons you can learn and ways to bring healing to your wounded heart.

# Chapter 4:  The Walking Dead— Are You One of Them?

No experience is a cause of success or failure. We do not suffer from the shock of our experiences, the so-called trauma, but we make out of them just what suits our purposes.

—Alfred Adler, Austrian psychologist (1870–1937)

We all carry pain; this is the human dilemma. Regardless of how wonderful the significant people in your life were, they were not perfect and did not and could not completely fill your emptiness. They could not completely fill the section in your heart chamber that was theirs to fill. They came into marriage and parenting with their own deficiencies and no matter how hard they tried to give you the best, somehow they fell short—just as you will with your children. Parenting is like golf: even if you are the very best, you are not perfect—just better than others.

When we seek to understand how our parents and significant others in our lives fell short of perfection, this is not to blame them. This is about choosing to understand them so we can understand ourselves and grow into more emotionally mature people.

Your task is to learn from the past and grow to a higher level of emotional health that you can pass on to your children and other family members. And besides, it will give you a certain amount of braggin' rights too: *Isn't it amazing that you and I became such a great and wonderful persons from such a dysfunctional family?*

You can blame *them* when *you* reach perfection as a spouse, parent, or grandparent. The simple fact is we are all part of the struggling human condition.

*Myths*

A myth is something people believe in even though the evidence does not support it. For example, members of a family might routinely say that the family is close-knit, yet take a closer look and you will see that they rarely talk to each other, gather together, or share anything of depth.

Somehow our society holds to and spreads myths like:

- Parents should know how to care for their children and do the right things.
- People should use common sense. Whatever that is!

  If common sense were common then we would all have it. There is no such thing as common sense. Ask three mothers how to discipline a child and see if you get a common response or "common sense." When most are using the phrase *common sense*, they are really saying, "You should think, believe, or see it like I do."
- Mothers have a natural maternal instinct. If so, why do they permit abortion to be performed on them? Why do they physically deprive or abuse their children? Why did the female inmate I counseled in prison who was

seen throwing her baby off the thirteenth floor balcony declare, "I loved my baby"? She was not insane or mentally ill.

- Parents should all be capable of unconditional love. Examine this myth by looking at yourself.

- Mothers are naturally more nurturing than fathers. This is just not necessarily so. We are too quick in our society to say men cannot be good caregivers and nurturers and then condemn them for not being what we believe they cannot be. This thinking is nuts.

- Mothers and fathers can meet all the emotional needs of their children.

- A single parent can do as good a job as a two-parent family. That may be true if the two-parent family is seriously dysfunctional. I think we would all agree that it takes two, a male and a female (that's a no-brainer), to make a child. So isn't that a strong message about the importance of having two healthy parents? I was raised in a single-parent family and my mother worked hard to raise us. But I missed a lot not having a father. I watched my buddies interact with their fathers and do things together. I knew I was missing out. Even when their fathers were angry at them or disciplined them, I didn't think, "I'm glad I don't have a father." Besides, who is going to fill the father chamber?

- Daycare can do as good a job at raising a child as a mother at home. You won't like this answer—but it is just not true. Oh yes, we have justified it by saying "quality time is more important than quantity." The problem is twofold. First, a mother cannot fill the mother chamber in the child's heart if they are not together. (I refer here to mother because she is typically the primary caregiver. I do recognize there are situations where the father is the one who stays home and raises the children.) Secondly, when the mother *is* home, there is little time for quality time. I challenge you to tell me families and society are better off today than in previous generations when mothers were at home with the children. Yes, I know there will be all kinds of reaction to these statements because they are not politically correct. But just because something is politically correct does not make it true.

## The Question

The question here is not whether some individuals have emotional pain and others do not. We have already established that we all have some degree of pain. The question, then, is, how much pain does each one of us carry and how do we chose to cope with it?

We live in a society where it is noble to wear our pain on our sleeves and declare that we are victims. Some get their fifteen minutes of fame making fools of themselves on TV just to publicize their excuse for living a low life. They come to the media, public events, or social groups to declare their pain and get others to sympathize with them so they do not have to accept responsibility for their behavior or change.

A friend of mine who has struggled with OCD (obsessive compulsive disorder) all his life told me he frequently came out of OCD meetings upset because all the group did was sit around and reinforce each other's excuses and symptoms. He told me he would often speak up and challenge the group to accept responsibility and work on their behaviors to try and overcome them. Soon he became *persona non grata* because he refused to participate in the victim game.

Some join groups so they can collectively market their victimization. Victim groups have become masters of the media. Those who play the victim game often want special treatment, especially if they have been caught in an embarrassing behavior or a criminal act. Elite rehab facilities have become the refuge of the rich and famous if they are caught in behavior that has the potential of jail time or might otherwise affect their career. They run immediately to the refuge to avoid the publicity and to show "remorse" and "apologize" and give the impression of change.

I challenge you to track the lives of some of these celebrities for a couple years afterward. I certainly believe in treatment for addictions and other destructive behaviors, but it seems that few seek help until they are exposed and their reputation and income is at risk.

If we go back a generation or two, we find our ancestors did not have to create ways to display pain. They had real suffering to contend with—the Great Depression, the Dust Bowl, and two World Wars. They did not use their pain as a badge of honor to win sympathy, be excused for their behavior, or find social power.

A little education into how they coped can be seen by viewing some old movies or some of the more recent ones that display the hard times. A couple good examples are *Oh, Brother Where Art Thou* and *Grapes of Wrath*.

Some researchers are constantly looking for dysfunctions in humanity so they can create new groups of people who can cluster together and label it a disease. Having a disease is much more palatable in our society than accepting responsibility for dealing with one's emotional pain. If we can label emotional pain a disease then we do not have to accept any responsibility, and we can take the latest pill that is highly promoted by the pharmaceutical companies.

Besides, if we label our emotional pain a disease then we can relegate it to a biological problem and not a mental or emotional problem. In our society it is much more noble to have a physical problem than an emotional one. I guess our society is not as accepting of emotional issues as we pretend to be.

We are still back in the dark ages in dealing with depression and other emotional responses. In our supposedly advanced society, we don't lock people up in filthy institutions and expect them to get better. We give them mind-numbing medications that lock them up inside themselves and expect them to get better *immediately*. Today, instead of institutionalizing persons in great emotional pain so we don't have to deal with them, we give them a pill. Once they have been given the magic pill, they are expected to fully function as though there were no problems.

As a therapist, I have frequently seen one spouse become very angry with the other spouse who was taking the antidepressant medication. He expected his partner to "be well," not have any mood swings, and to have normal libido and energy. So we have gone from failing to compassionately deal with our hurting family members to failing to help our family. Is this progress?

*Let me be clear!* I do acknowledge there are some real biological disorders, like schizophrenia, which do require medication to assist functioning. Before you react too strongly, read on.

## A Disease or An Illness

Our society is failing to correctly distinguish between a disease and an illness. We are using the terms synonymously and they are not synonymous. Dr. David Keith, a leader in understanding the interaction of psychotherapy and pharmacology has properly defined the difference:

> Disease is a disruption of biological structure of function, which the practitioner, with superior specialized knowledge, can diagnose, that is, measure and name. A disease can be objectively defined in unambiguous, nonmetaphorical language. Examples

are pneumonia, diabetes, fractured tibia, lymphoma. The practitioner institutes treatment that mitigates or eradicates the symptoms and signs.

Illness refers to a much more ambiguous territory and is harder to understand, for a good reason. Illness in [Arthur] Kleinman's system refers to the cultural or interpersonal manifestation of a disease. Illness is shared by all involved with the afflicted—patient, family, and practitioner. Thus illness exists between persons; it is multipersonal. Illness is a problem of the whole person, not of a single organ or organ system.... Illness is not treated; it is contextualized— that is, it is placed in a context of relationships and events. Illness, because it is dynamic and unpredictable, is not namable.[8]

He also states:

For example, we describe depression as disease "like diabetes." It is the result of "chemical imbalance." Now, in fact, there is no measurable chemical imbalance, as there is in diabetes. But in the logic of modern psychiatry, because some symptoms of depression respond to treatment with chemicals, the illness is defined as a chemical imbalance."[9]

Statistically, it is clear that most depression is reactive to some problem or unresolved life event.[10] Depression is a normal human reaction to loss, tragedy, abuse, and so on. Let's acknowledge this and deal with the source of the real pain through therapy rather than refuse to accept responsibility by running to prescription drugs or street addictions. These only mask the problem. Often the end result is broken marriages or relationships or a less than satisfactory life.

Many of you are living lives of secret desperation when a little good professional assistance will help you to live a fulfilling life.

You may have seen the old cartoon joke that pictures a gravestone that says, "Died at forty buried at eighty." There are millions of walking dead in our society. Are you one of them? If you are, gather your courage and seek good professional help to deal with the source of your pain rather than trying to mask it, which you know does not work. You know that the means you are using to mask the pain is just producing more pain. The results of masking are often constant frustration, a sense of helplessness, and broken relationships that ultimately end in your being physically and emotionally isolated. The result of not dealing with the *source* of pain is always more pain.

Stop dealing with the symptoms. Deal with the cause. If you had a serious infection in your finger, would you allow this to grow to your hand and arm until you had to have your arm amputated?

*Pain and Loss*

Our premise is that most of our emotional pain comes from emptiness in the chambers of our heart. One may live reasonably well with empty chambers by denying their emptiness. However, this emptiness is often exposed when there is some loss or tragedy that makes one aware of their emptiness.

Daily we hear of someone suddenly killing another person or persons, and we are shocked again. We should not be shocked. There are millions of empty vessels walking the streets of our cities. When the right combination of loss, stress, or disaster intersects and the person cannot contain the pain, he strikes out, often with disastrous consequences.

If you are one of these, you know it. You are important, so seek help today!

One day when I was making my rounds in the prison, I was paged to go immediately to solitary confinement. The correctional officer in the unit informed me that we had a new admission who was very distressed. When I entered the cell I encountered a man in his fifties who was totally emotionally distraught. All he could get out amidst his extreme anguish was "I just killed everything I have ever worked for." He had just shot his teenage daughter and her boyfriend.

As I came to know this man, a first-generation immigrant, I learned he had never harmed anyone and did not even have a parking ticket. He worked two jobs to provide his family with everything he never had. One day when he came home his daughter and her boyfriend were sitting on the sofa talking; they were not even being affectionate. The father, in attempting to be protective, had previously told her many times he did not like the boyfriend and not to go with him. In a fit of rage he went into his bedroom and came out with a shotgun and killed them both.

Friends, there is repressed pain in all of us and we need to uncover it and bring healing to our heart, for in the right combination circumstances, we, too, can do something destructive to ourselves, our loved ones, or even strangers. This will change our life forever. We may not physically kill anyone, but we may seriously wound someone's self-esteem, or our relationship with him. We may not kill him with a shot-gun, but we can slowly kill him emotionally with our cruel words or behavior.

When you experience a loss or some other painful experience and your reaction greatly exceeds the situation, the overreaction comes from your previous unresolved pain or emptiness. For example, if you find that a friend has betrayed you, it is normal to be angry, upset, or even a bit depressed. However, if your reaction is one of being totally crushed or devastated, if it puts you into a deep depression and immobilizes you, then this is overreactive and the additional emotional response is likely coming from preexisting hurt and pain. Imagine a scale of one to five (one being the lowest and five highest); if it is appropriate to react as a two but you react as a five, the excess stems from your unresolved past hurt or emptiness.

Or perhaps you accidentally walk in front of someone in the grocery line; it is appropriate for them to politely point it out. But if they scream and yell and pull out a gun, this is definitely overreaction. If you are late picking up your spouse and he or she verbally shreds you, the issue is not just about you being late; it is a resurrection of some previous hurt.

Resurrecting previous hurts or emptiness on an unsuspecting spouse is probably one of the major causes of divorce. The unsuspecting spouse goes away shaking his head, confused, saying, "I don't deserve this." And they probably didn't.

Susan went through a difficult divorce. She lost her home, stepchildren, employment, and had to move to another city to pursue her career. It was appropriate for her to experience depression. However, she became very depressed, became self-destructive, bulimic, and excessively sexually promiscuous. When we looked into her life we discovered many empty chambers. Her father had been much less than a good father, her mother had not been strong in nurturing, she did not have any children of her own, she was an only child, and had always suffered from low self-esteem. Her divorce exposed all her emptiness. She did not have one emotionally strong heart chamber to draw upon to get her through the difficult divorce.

When she looked inside her heart it was quite empty. This made her recovery much harder and longer than if she had received good nurturing early in life and had the joy of being a parent and had developed her own self-worth rather than relying on her husband to give her identity and esteem.

When there is loss, the question is not so much "What did I lose?" The appropriate questions are, "What is left?" and "What does the loss mean to me?" The loss can be traumatic, but if there is a healthy heart to begin with, the sufferer will weather the storm much better than a person who finds an empty heart.

Several years ago I counseled a couple who left their two small children with a responsible adult, a sister-in-law, and went on their first vacation alone since becoming parents. While they were away, their two small children perished in a house fire. Obviously, this couple was devastated, but they coped much better than one could have imagined because they both had healthy hearts and a great marriage. It was amazing to watch them recover and soon start a new family. They did not hold anger and resentment toward the sister in-law, who was not negligent. It was just a tragic accident.

Life is difficult, especially if you have limited emotional reserves to draw on. Now is the time to examine your heart, resolve the emotional pain and build a strong emotional base, because I can guarantee you that you are going to need it.

Financial planners say you should have at least six months cash reserves for the unexpected. Do you have fire insurance on your home because you are planning on setting your house on fire? No, but in case there is a fire, you will not lose all your investment. Likewise, you need to build strong emotional reserves for the unexpected because the unexpected *will* happen.

*Why Do You Keep Your Pain?*

We have established that we all have emotional hurt and pain. Now the question is "Why do you chose to keep the pain of the past?" If you are keeping your old hurts and pain and are not working on building a health emotional life, then you must be getting something out of your pain or you would not keep it. Each time I say this to a client, he gives me a puzzled look. The response often is, "Why would I want to keep this pain?" As we begin to examine it, he soon sees his reason for keeping it.

- It could be they enjoy being resentful because it keeps others away from them.
- Or they keep the anger because they feel more powerful and less vulnerable.
- Or the pain gets them pity.
- Or it is their excuse for being unkind or addicted.
- Or they have nurtured it for so long giving it up would be like losing their identity.
- And there are many more possibilities.

We live in a society where it is a badge of honor to wear your pain externally and always be ready to tell your story of abuse or neglect. In some TV shows or church testimonials, it is about who can tell the worst abuse story. It is rarely about how "I overcame and I enjoy my life" now. No, the worse the story, the more acceptance and recognition one receives.

It is usually easy to identify why you've kept the destructive emotion. The difficult part is choosing to give it up and live without it. Believe it or not, emotional pain is empowering. In some ways it is difficult to carry it about every day, and in other ways, you feel empowered and ready for battle.

Some clients enter into a therapy with the attitude of not to change or to be changed but to convince the therapist that they have a major problem, and if they believe they can convince the therapist then they can convince anyone and maintain the right to continue as they are.

Yes, you, like everyone else have emotional hurt and pain. So you are not so unique after all. The question still confronts you. Do you choose to remain in your pain and chose a dysfunctional way to deal with your pain. Or do you chose to rise above the hurt and move toward becoming the healthy self?

*Life-Changing Questions to Ponder*

- Am I going to choose to keep my pain and use it as my weapon of choice?
- Am I going to pursue forgiveness and healing?
- Am I going to fill my life with positive emotional food?
- Am I going to be prepared for the crises that *will* come into my life?
- Am I going to remain emotionally destitute?
- Am I going to continue to live in self-pity because my family of origin failed me?
- Am I going to pass my pain on to my children and grandchildren?
- Am I going to start building my emotional reserves today?

You are an adult. You have already made many life choices, like your career, your relationships, your residence, and many more. Now is the time to choose to live a healthy emotional life. It is your life; it is your choice.

# Chapter 5: Meet Your Monkeys

Pain hurts. And we don't like pain and hurt so we attempt many dysfunctional remedies to make the pain go away. The problem is that the homemade remedies we choose usually only mask the pain, while creating other problems. The medical term for a secondary illness caused while attempting to cure the original illness is iatrogenic. Often the patient is left with a physical condition that is worse than the original diagnosis, or, at best, a second illness that must be treated.

The majority of emotional problems are iatrogenic in that they are the result of trying to cure the original emotional distress. Typically, the original emotional pain is not relieved and the secondary emotional response is worse, or only compounds the primary pain.

For example, when someone has hurt you badly, you build a wall around yourself and say, "I will never let anyone hurt me again." In building a fortress you not only keep others out but you have walled yourself in. Soon it starts to get lonely inside your fortress. You must decide to either open the gate and go out, let others in, or close down your emotions and block out the loneliness. If you chose to block others out, your isolating cycle intensifies until you are lonely, cold, bitter, and empty. Before you know it, you live in a very lonely, small world inside your fortress, all alone without friends. The next stage is you try to pass off the lonely pain by saying, "I don't need anyone." Down and down the cycle goes.

*Four Psychological Monkeys*

Remember the old expression, "I have a monkey on my back"? Fear, anger, guilt, and inadequacy have been called the four psychological monkeys—a manifestation of something negative controlling you, dominating you, or keeping you from being free to be yourself. The monkey is notorious for its constant annoying chatter. We want to shut it up, but we can't. It chatters day and night, whether we are alone or with others. We want to shake it off, but it is very adept at hanging on and digging its claws into us. It inhibits our movement and freedom. It destroys our relationships because it dominates us and we are afraid to respond or reach out.

You have a monkey on your back. The questions to ask yourself are:

- Which monkey(s) is it?
- How powerful is it?
- How much is it controlling you?

Most of the emotional reactions we adopt to protect us from emotional pain can be traced back to one or more of these four psychological monkeys.

*The Fear Monkey*

Fear is both good and destructive at the same time. It is a natural emotional defense we are all endowed with. Fear keeps us alive everyday. It is good to be afraid of walking out into the street in front of an oncoming truck, or stepping out of an airplane at thirty thousand feet without a parachute (or even with one). It keeps us from drinking out of a bottle labeled with the skull and crossbones on it, or putting our hands on the red hot stove burner. It keeps us from criminal acts because we are fearful of being caught and going to prison.

But fear that is nurtured and fed grows into a monster that controls and dominates you rather than protecting you. Soon the fear monkey is on your back chattering to you all the time to be careful, look out, don't trust, and so on. Soon the symptoms consume, control, and make you miserable. Now the fear monkey is in charge of your life rather than you being in charge.

Then fear morphs into all types of strange creatures that don't look a thing like their parent. Assume someone becomes terrified of the dark and they nurture the fear. It could morph into fear of going outdoors, fear of spiders, fear of flying, and fear of eating, which could become anorexia or bulimia. It could become OCD (Obsessive Compulsive Disorder). This new creature bears no resemblance to the original source; it becomes much harder to recognize and resolve. This is why we need to address and resolve our fears before they become difficult to recognize and take over our hearts, bodies, and our lives. This is why we need to identify the monkey while it is still recognizable.

Anxiety is not an emotion. It is an emotional reaction to fear. When our fear alarm bells go off inside, it triggers our system to get ready to run or fight. Adrenalin is triggered so that we have an abundance of extra energy for protection.

If you don't use up this energy force to run from the bear or fight it, you will start to shake and tremble. Your body is not equipped for this type of reaction, where the adrenalin is triggered and you need to go into action but can't. Often you must stay at your desk or some other nonphysical activity.

When your grandmother felt anxiety she beat the rug with a wire whip, chopped a cord of wood, carried buckets of water, or slopped the hogs. Today, we are told to go to the gym and burn it off. Few of us do, resulting in the adrenalin eating us up inside and destroying our physical, emotional, and relational health.

I often compare anxiety to starting a car, shifting it into neutral, putting your foot on the accelerator and pressing it all the way to the floor. The car shakes and roars and immediately you hear your father yell, "Don't do that, you will destroy the motor!" If you put the car into gear and accelerate, no harm is done because you are using the energy.

All humans are masters at converting fear to anger. When your little child runs out into the street you scream, yell, and grab him by the arm, and probably starting spanking him. You have just converted fear to anger. Others may not see your fear, but they are likely to see observe your anger, which came from the fear. Teenagers don't understand why parents are so angry when they come home much later than the curfew. They try to explain where they were, but all they get is anger from the terrified parent. Neither the teen nor the parent has a clue that fear has been converted into anger.

When you have been hurt by someone or by life's circumstances and you hold the emotional pain inside, it is common to become chronically angry. You chose to convert your fear to anger to protect yourself from being hurt again. Anger is your army of defenders, pushed to the frontlines by fear.

*The Anger Monkey*

An old legend from the fourth century, is the story of Damocles an excessively flattering courtier in the court of Dionysius in Italy. Damocles often expressed his jealousy of the king Dionysius. So one day the king offered to switch places with Damocles for a day, so he could experience first hand what it was like to be in a place of power. In the evening, a great banquet was held and Damocles was greatly enjoying being waited upon like the king. Near the end of the meal Damocles looked up and noticed a large sharpened sword hanging by a single strand of horsehair directly above his head. Immediately, he lost all interest in the fine foods and beautiful girls and asked to be relieved of the role of king.

The Sword of Damocles is sometimes used as a symbol of peril faced by those in positions of power. More generally, it is used to denote a precarious situation. Especially one in which the onset of tragedy is restrained only by a delicate trigger or chance.

When you keep your volatile anger to protect yourself, it is hanging precariously, only a horsehair away from destroying you or someone else. When you hurt someone else with your anger, you are also bringing hurt and possible destruction to yourself, whether you recognize it or not.

When you keep your volatile anger to defend yourself, you are wearing an invisible sword in an invisible scabbard on your side. You know it is there and so does everyone else. When they start to threaten you, you rattle your saber and if they don't back off, you pull it out and wave it in the air. At this point most people *will* back off. However, occasionally there is some fool who doesn't see your sword or fails to heed your warning so you stab him with it.

This whole sequence started because someone betrayed you or hurt you in some way. You felt the emotional hurt and pain and decided you never wanted to feel that way again, so you equipped yourself with your sword and are always prepared for battle. The guy who gets stabbed never knew what hit him or why. He goes away more confused than ever. You have just successfully protected your fear and converted your fear into anger to protect yourself from being hurt again. There is only one problem: you have just lost self-control and harmed another friend—or is it now a former friend or spouse?

Many addictions are rooted in fear. When fear gets triggered, the anxiety starts to take over, so the fearful person eats, shops, drinks, snorts, looks at porn, has sex, cuts himself, and so on and so on. And when it is unbearable, he might even kill himself.

Remember, much of your pain is coming from the deficiency in the chambers of your heart. If you were not given safety, security, and predictability as a child, you may have chronic anxiety that is manifested in different forms that in no way resemble the original cause. Check the mother and father chambers of your heart; see if they lack the gift of love, safety, security, and predictability.

It appears that every generation has a primary monkey it must contend with. Go back a generation and the major monkey was a sense of inadequacy, especially in women. Our mothers commonly underestimated their abilities.

In this generation it seems the monkey that runs rampant is the anger monkey. Our society is riddled through and through with expressions of anger. The movies, news, and behavior we see each day is not just anger, but extreme anger. We seem to love it so much we watch endless hours of TV to get our fill of violence—and then wonder why we have to take a sleeping aid. We can't wait to watch the latest news to see who killed whom. We are addicted to and intoxicated with anger and violence. Some of the anger may have originally come from fear or anxiety, but it has been around for so long that now it has a life of its own and regenerates itself and is passed from person to person and generation to generation.

## Causes of Anger

To simplify our understanding of the causes of anger, let's examine the four primary causes of anger.

- When someone or something *withholds* from you what you thought was rightfully yours. (Examples: when love, affection, respect, a promotion, a raise, are withheld.)
- When someone *withdraws* something from you what you previously had and believed was rightfully yours. (Examples: you lose your job, or benefits are reduced, a relationship breaks up, loss of health, your house burns down, someone steals your valuables.)
- When someone *blocks* your goal. (Examples: when your promotion is blocked, you are refused a job or entrance into a university, the idiot who cut in front of you on the highway or drives too slow so you are late for your appointment, etc.)
- When you are being threatened. Again, we are referring to converting fear into anger.

Most of us can quickly identify overt anger when it is expressed in the obvious ways. These expressions of anger can be from mild to extreme. The most commonly identified expressions of anger are:

- Verbal expressions like screaming, yelling, arguing, verbal abuse, threatening, and the like.
- Physical abuse of slapping, hitting, punching or worse violence, including rape.

While these expressions are serious and we need to take note of them, there are many subtle expressions of anger that can be just as destructive. Often people choose less obvious expressions of anger, because it is not safe to properly express anger and hurt, so they must deny it and bottle it up. Here is a short list of expressions of anger.

*Subtle Expressions of Anger*

- Depression. Depression is commonly referred to as anger turned in. The great majority of depression is rooted in unresolved anger, when you allow the anger to simmer internally because of some loss or injustice or perceived injustice. You may allow it to simmer for so long that you have forgotten the original hurt that produced the anger. And now all you know is that you are depressed. In our society, it all too common to want to take a pill rather than find the source and resolve it. Depression is like a fire alarm bell warning you that there is a potentially serious problem. But you don't like to hear the alarm bell, so you turn it off with a pill. Turning off the bell does not mean there is no problem. Now the small fire has the potential to become a five-alarm fire that is much more destructive and much more difficult to put out. As Plutarch, the second century philosopher, said of the depressed person, "He looks on himself as a man whom the Gods hate and pursue with their anger."
- Emotional Coldness. Have you ever noticed how some people are emotionally cold? You touch them, if you dare, and you don't feel any emotional warmth. They don't laugh, hug, or engage emotionally. They are like an iceberg. You see the obvious piece of the iceberg but hidden underneath lays a mass of coldness much greater than you can imagine. The problem with anger is that most humans cannot compartmentalize it. Once it starts, it grows like a cancer through the entire system if it is not identified and treated. For example, if you

have a deficiency in your mother or father chamber and you have unforgiven anger toward them, you cannot contain the anger in those chambers. The anger from one chamber soon spreads to other chambers. It does not take long for the anger to migrate to all relationships and your entire view of life itself. Anger can grow like a fungus. It quickly propagates itself. The final result is an emotionally cold human who neither gives nor receives love and compassion.

- Manipulation. The master manipulators of the world all have a reservoir of anger. Manipulation is the act of controlling or playing upon others without their full knowledge or consent. You do it for your own selfish gain. The classic study on manipulators is *Man the Manipulator* by Dr. Everett Shostrom. His research clearly shows that all manipulators are angry; they don't trust themselves and they don't trust you. I once had a client who was sent to me because she was an extreme manipulator at work and home. After a couple sessions I confronted her on a manipulative move she tried on me. She began to cry, so I waited a bit and then said, "I don't know if you are sincere and remorseful about your behavior or you are being manipulative." She said, "I don't know either." And I never knew if that was also a manipulative move. One of the major problems for those who are around manipulators is that you never know when they are being genuine.
- Passive-aggressive behavior. Passive-aggressive people refuse to be direct, open, honest, and appropriate about what they want. They don't walk into a room with confidence but bring with them a sense of disapproval and gloom so that others are careful about how they approach them. They manipulate others to make the decisions and then directly or indirectly find a way to show disapproval or blame others when it

does not turn out well. They are masters at making others feel and accept responsibility for things that are not their responsibility.

- Sexual Expressions. Rape, sexual abuse, impotence, exhibitionism, and frigidity are all subtle expressions of anger. Frigid individuals seal up their sexuality and come across as extremely emotionally cold and closed. The intriguing thing about human sexuality is that it is woven through the fabric of our being. We cannot separate it from who we are. If you shut down your sexuality and become frigid you simultaneously close down all your warmth and sensitivity. It is commonly accepted that when you are unable to express your anger, you usually have difficulty in feeling your love and being sexuality appropriate. When you admit it and deal with your anger, you usually automatically turn on a healthy sexuality as well.

- Saccharin Sweet. This is one of my favorites because this person is rarely seen as an angry person. These are the individuals who are so sweet it makes you sick to your stomach. Their sweetness is artificial—saccharin sweet. They completely repress their anger and could not express any overt form of anger, hurt, or disappointment if their life depended on it. Even when you run over them with a truck they get up and apologize for being in the way.

- Crazy Clean. These are usually women who are excessive in their housecleaning. When I taught on this subject, most women would quickly and jokingly say, "This is not me, so I must not be angry." In one session I was teaching, a woman almost jumped out of her chair and said I was describing her mother-in-law. She explained, "If you walk across her carpet she will get out the vacuum and immediately follow behind you. When you set down a dirty dish she immediately grabs it and washes it." This is a very deceptive way to control and it looks socially acceptable. However, it makes everyone feel very uncomfortable. Many years ago I read a Dear Abby column in which a woman described how her friend even waxed the toilet seats.

- Addictions. It is common to find deep-seated anger in people who are addicted to food, drink, drugs, shopping, sex, or you name the addiction. The anger can be directed at self or others.
- Extreme Controllers. These are individuals who both covertly and overtly attempt to control everything and everyone. One of their favorite lines is, "I am only doing it for your good." They sometimes come across as protectors. Again, they say they are "only looking out for you." All mental health professionals know that when someone says he is only protecting someone else, the truth is he is really protecting himself. Protectors can be very dangerous. They include the likes of Adolph Hitler and Jim Jones, the infamous cult leader who took his following to Guyana and fed them poisoned Kool Aid. Be alert to those who want to protect you.
- Bulimia or Anorexia. It is not uncommon to find these individuals with deep seated anger. They often feel they have no control over their lives and this is one way they can control themselves and their destiny. In young troubled children, we often see constant soiling and wetting as an expression of anger. This is their only sense of control over their lives and no one can stop them.
- And More Expressions:
  - Blaming others, like "you made me angry"
  - Acting out, which is taking out your anger on someone other than the one you are angry at

- Kick-me games, where you set yourself up to have others abuse you
- Chronic physical illnesses
- Jealousy

The question is not whether you get angry. The question is whether you harbor anger and then turn it on yourself or others in a destructive way. The descriptions above are some examples of how people act out anger. Don't automatically assume that someone has great amounts of anger just because he expresses it occasionally. It is the frequency and intensity of acting out anger that is noteworthy.

By now you have probably labeled all your family and friends (except yourself) with how they express their anger. Resist the temptation to become the family therapist! This is intended for you to take a look at yourself and understand how a deficit in one of your heart chambers can fill your life with anger. We will examine how to deal with inappropriate expressions of anger in the chapters ahead.

### The Guilt Monkey

Is this your favorite monkey? Do you go around feeling guilty or saying how guilty you feel? Does this monkey have a grip on you and control your life? Let's examine it. The first step to freedom is understanding and acknowledging your monkey. If you understand how your guilt monkey controls you and makes you miserable, then you can learn how to tame it.

Guilt is feeling a sense of remorse for violating society's rules or the personal rules of yourself or someone else. There are times that we are guilty but don't have a sense of remorse because we did not know we violated a law. Remember when the police officer pulled you over for running a stop sign that you really did not see? You were guilty even though you did not *feel* guilty. Contrast that to how you felt when you knew you did not stop. You were guilty and possibly had guilty feelings. Most good police officers can see the guilt in a guilt-ridden person regardless of what they say.

Some of your grandparents would have never gone to a movie on Sunday afternoon because they would have had strong guilt feelings. And grandmother would have never worn slacks, especially to church. Most likely you do all the above and other things your parents or grandparents would never have done, and you don't feel any guilt. Guilt changes and evolves in families and society.

The capacity and intensity with which we acknowledge and feel guilt is developed in us by the age of six or seven. We are not born with a list of rights and wrongs preprogrammed in our brains. We each learn about guilt from our significant caregivers. Some parents pour great amounts of guilty statements and feelings into their small children's heart chambers. The child grows up with his heart chambers full of guilt, so he takes responsibility and feels guilty for everything that happens around him. When one person has made a mistake and someone else says, "I am soooo sorry," it is like that person is taking onto himself guilt that is not his. Often there is no need for anyone to feel guilty, it just happened, and there was no moral issue involved. Some people feel guilty if it rains at the family picnic, as though they were somehow responsible!

Early in life we are taught by our parents what to feel guilty about and the degree of guilt we should feel. Sometimes we accept what they are doing to us. Other times we reject it because we don't have the same sense of guilt as they do. Since no two adults were raised exactly the same or accepted their parents teaching identically, it is common for married couples to get into arguments about guilt. To illustrate, the wife will say, "I feel so guilty about what happened" and husband will say, "I don't." Then she will say, "How can you be so insensitive?" Now the war is on. The wife then converts her sense of guilt into anger and the husband shrugs his shoulders and walks off. Or perhaps he has an affair and apologizes, but does not express the level of guilt she expects him to have. She thinks, "If I did that I could never live with myself" or "I would show more remorse than he did, so I guess he is not sorry. And that means he will probably do it again."

Watch a mother try to get her little boy to say, "I'm sorry I hit my sister." Maybe he is not sorry and maybe he is glad he did it and felt justified. She should not try to force him into feeling guilty. Instead, she should teach him about proper behavior and how to treat others. A "guilt whipping" will most likely dull his sense of guilt, rather than sharpen it.

The other dangerous extreme is to never feel or acknowledge guilt. Yes, there are a large number of people in our society, mostly men, who rarely or never have a guilty feeling. When they have been properly evaluated by a professional and have been determined to truly feel no guilt, they are called psychopaths or sociopaths. Typically these are very bright, articulate, perfectionist, manipulative, good-looking, and well-groomed males. Many are professionals. Don't think "dirty old men in rain coats." An excellent orthodontist that I knew socially revealed to me that he was diagnosed as a psychopath. He said he never felt guilty about anything. He stayed out of serious trouble by considering the consequences of his actions. He said, "I don't step far over the line because I don't want to go to jail and lose my great life." Like many others, he controls himself by evaluating the consequences of what he could lose if he got caught.

I will never forget the day I went into the solitary confinement cell of one of my captive clients. I saw him several times a week for several months while he was going through trial for raping and murdering a little boy. The previous night he had been found guilty and sentenced to life in prison.

When I entered his cell, he had his back to me and I called him by name and asked him what he was doing. He replied, "Drawing a schematic for a radio receiver." Though I knew he was a psychopath, I was still shocked. What would you have been doing and feeling if you had just been found guilty of his crime and sentenced to life? As I pursued the conversation I asked, "Do you feel guilty for what you have done?" He replied without emotion, "No, in fact if my mother came in here now, I could kill her and feel nothing. I only regret what I have done because now I have to spend life in prison and I cannot be out on the street." And of course I thought, *And I am glad you are going to spend life in prison and not be on the street.*

You may be wondering how he became a psychopath. He and his sister were adopted at a young age and he never had the natural mother and father parent chamber in his heart filled, even though he had good adoptive parents. Because of the deficit in the parental chambers of his heart he had great emotional pain, which he turned to anger and rage from an early age. Interestingly, his sister chose another response to her pain and became a very delightful Christian woman; she was broken-hearted and felt guilty because of what her brother had done.

A big mistake most people make is to assume that others around them feel the same degree of guilt over the same things as they do. Chances are that two people don't feel the same degree of guilt over the same things.

Having a hyperactive (overactive) or hypoactive (under-active) thyroid will put you on emotional highs and lows until you get the correct medication to level it out. An overactive guilt complex or underactive sense of guilt is not healthy either. You may need to do some work on your guilt issues if this is the monkey that is on your back.

Most mental health professionals will agree that at least 90 percent of our guilt is anger at ourselves for not measuring up to our own values and expectations. Thus, many people with a hyperactive sense of guilt come across as very angry. They are so angry at themselves they cannot contain the anger, so it is spewed all over those around them. Then it is a vicious cycle: now they feel more guilt because of the way they treated others, which produces more anger at self, which comes out on others. And so the cycle grows.

This is very similar to the alcoholic syndrome. A person feels inadequate or guilty, so he drinks to mask the feelings. Then when he is sober he becomes aware of how he hurt others when he was drinking, and then he feels guilty, so he drinks again to mask the guilty feelings. And so the vicious cycle goes.

If you have committed some offense and are carrying guilt for what you have done, there is hope. In chapter six you'll learn how to manage your monkeys. If this guilt monkey is controlling your life, now is the time to get some help. There is hope that you can level out your life and live a more fulfilling life. If you have an underactive sense of guilt, you need to take a serious look at yourself and develop a constructive moral compass for your life.

*The Inadequacy Monkey*

It's our parents' job to give us our self-esteem. From the time of our birth, parents are responsible for helping us to understand we are persons of worth and value, and that our value is not predicated on what we do but who we are. It is not a black and white issue, as our parents will either genuinely love us in a healthy way, or will be incapable of giving us the love we need. There is a range of loving that spans from unconditional love to conditional love.

In chapter two, we learned that our parents are responsible for filling the hole in our hearts. If our mothers and fathers were given unconditional love by their parents, then it is much easier for them to pass it on to us. If, however, they did not receive the appropriate unconditional love, they must make a conscious effort to learn how to love us unconditionally.

Unconditional love accepts and loves a child as a person of worth and value, without placing conditions on his performance. Good parenting separates the child's personal value from his behavior. Good parents say, "I love you, but I do not approve of your behavior." It is that simple.

Our self-esteem is formed from what our parents say to us and how they say it. If, when we bring home a grade of ninety on a school exam and the first thing they say is "Where are the other ten points," it is clear that their love is conditional on what we achieve, not who we are. If, on the other hand, they are our supporters and boosters no matter how well we do, then we will feel unconditionally loved, which in turn goes a long way toward giving us a positive self-esteem. Proper unconditional love will say, "Let's see how we can help you improve."

I never cease to be amazed at how many apparently good parents are quick to point out their child's faults and expect to motivate them to do better next time. The fact is, if a parent is quick to point out all the things a child does poorly in trying to clean up his room, for example, rather than first identifying his good efforts and the specifics of what he did well, this will be seen by the child as criticism, and the compliment will be meaningless. Next time he will not do better but will put in less effort (unless he is terrified of the parent). This, of course, is not positive parenting.

Let's be very clear that unconditional love does not mean allowing one's children to do as they please and go undisciplined. Kids are smart. They know that proper discipline is a sign of love. Allowing one's children to do as they please is not love, because a selfish child will have few friends. When the child becomes an undisciplined adult, they will find life very difficult because they will have few friends and find it quite difficult to have a meaningful career. No one loves to be around selfish, self-centered children or adults.

It is critical, as well, that parents speak to and treat children with respect. If parents want a child to learn respect, then they will need to model it. Children are human beings and need to be seen and treated as such.[12]

Many years ago I lived in a condominium next door to a young couple. They seemed like a decent young couple and we enjoyed each other's company. When their baby entered the "wonderful twos" stage, I could hear, through concrete walls, the mother yelling at the little girl, "You dirty little rat." She did not strike the child or neglect her in any way. But what do you think calling a child a dirty little rat would do to her fragile self-esteem? So I found the right moment to speak to the husband in a caring way about what I was hearing and how it would affect the child. I do believe that he spoke to his wife about this because soon the yelling diminished and disappeared.

When we feel inadequate we often refuse to try new things and are very uncomfortable meeting new people and making new friends. This results in not fully experiencing the joy of life.

One of the great misunderstandings of self-esteem is that people with strong self-esteem are arrogant, proud, or obnoxious. The fact is those who are arrogant, proud, or obnoxious have *low*, not high, self-esteem. They are over-compensating for their low sense of self-worth. You can usually tell those who are overcompensating because you find yourself thinking, "I want to cut him down to size," or "I want to let the air out of his balloon," or "he certainly thinks a lot of himself."

A feeling of inadequacy is the mother of depression, because you can so easily get down on yourself.

Carl Rogers, the great psychotherapist who developed his counseling philosophy on unconditional positive regard, wrote, "If I can provide a certain type of relationship, the other person will discover within himself the capacity to use that relationship for growth and change and personal development will occur." He went on to say the key elements to building that relationship are being "genuine," "having warm regard for him as a person of unconditional self-worth," "sensitive empathy," and "transparency"; then the individual will find within himself the ability "to move forward toward maturity."[13]

This model of psychotherapy works. It will work for you as a spouse, parent, or grandparent as you seek to deposit positive emotional nourishment in the heart chamber of your loved one.

If you were not given the gift of positive self-esteem it is not too late. You can develop it so that you will feel better about yourself. We will address what you can do in chapter six.

*Jumping Monkeys*

Have you ever watched a cage full of monkeys at the zoo? They don't just sit in one place but are constantly jumping around and trading places. They can be quite hyper.

Your psychological monkeys are similar.

- When your primary monkey is fear it can jump and become anger or then guilt because of something you have done.
- When your primary monkey is anger it can jump and become inadequacy.
- When your primary monkey is guilt it can change and become the anger or inadequacy monkey.

- When your primary monkey is inadequacy it can be seen as fear or anger.

The principal is that although you have one primary monkey, it can take on the characteristics of another monkey for a period of time. However, your primary monkey is always present and directing your feelings and behavior.

It is told that an old native Indian man once said, "I have two dogs fighting in me all the time, a black dog and a white dog. The dog that I feed is the one that wins the battle of the day." You have four monkeys fighting to take control of your life. The one that you feed is the one that will control you that day.

*Monkey Questions*

- Which monkey is your favorite?
- Which monkey is your second favorite?
- Which monkey sometimes takes on the characteristics of another monkey?
- Which monkey controls and dominates you the most?
- Which monkey brings you the greatest pain?
- Which monkey do you feed because it protects you?

The final and most important question is this: will you continue to let your monkey (or monkeys) run wild and dominate your life or do you want to tame it?

Don't kill it—learn how to tame it.

# Chapter 6: Managing Your Monkeys

Do not kill your monkeys. Manage them!
You need all four monkeys to keep you safe and moral. If you attempt to kill or stifle your anger monkey, the anger will find a way of coming out in a different form. The disguised ways, which we described in chapter five, may be either physical or emotional or a combination of both.

Did you answer the questions at the end of the chapter?

- Which monkey controls and dominates you the most?
- Which monkey brings you the greatest pain?

Now read how to manage the four monkeys, giving particular attention to your favorite or favorites.

## Managing Your Fear Monkey

In small doses, fear is a lifesaver. In large doses, fear is a life killer.

Your fear monkey will keep you from doing foolish things that can kill you—or at least make your life, or some one else's, miserable. For example, it can inhibit you from drinking poison, or putting all your assets on one number and spinning the wheel in Vegas, or going ninety miles an hour through a school zone.

However, most people have too much fear. It keeps me, for example, from enjoying either scuba or sky diving, where I could see the wonders of the world and expand my horizons.

A good balance of fear makes us aware of the risks and calls us to take precautions but enjoy new experiences.

What would you do if you were not afraid?

- Would you try a new career?
- Would you start your own business?
- Would you go back to college?
- Would you talk to people you avoid?
- Would you travel in an airplane or learn to fly one?
- Would you forgive those who have offended you and give them another chance?

Fill in the sentence. If I were not afraid I would———————————————.

As I wrote in the previous chapter, anxiety is the manifestation of fear. Do you have to take a pill to control your anxiety? If so, why don't you become courageous and face your fear so you can overcome the inhibitor?

Did you know that most fears are irrational? For example:

- Fear of flying: you are more likely to be killed in a car accident.
- Public speaking: when was the last time you saw an audience throw things at the speaker or boo him off the stage?

- Building a new relationship: what is the worst that can happen? Rejection. And if you *are* rejected, will you die or just experience some emotional pain?

I love a good dose of pain (for others of course, not for me) because it gives you a chance to break out of the status quo and grow. You'll learn more about this in chapter seven.

Which will it be? Fear that keeps you from reaching your highest potential, or fear that gives you a false sense of safety? When we are controlled by fear, there is no safe position.

*Managing Your Anger Monkey*

We are created with the ability to become angry. Like many things, anger is healthy in small quantities. Once we start to overuse a good thing, it becomes destructive. For example, food, aspirin, prescription drugs, working, sunbathing, exercise, staying at home, or shopping can shift from necessary and healthy to destructive and unhealthy.

The key question to determine whether something is healthy or unhealthy is, "Are you managing and controlling the monkey, or does it control you?"

When you manage your anger, you are using it appropriately to defeat injustice and potential harm to yourself and others. If someone attacks you or a helpless innocent person, I hope you become angry and shift to the protection stance. However, you must restrain your monkey so that you only use the necessary amount of force. Don't let the monkey have free reign or it will cause you more heartache. Don't physically harm someone if all you have to do is restrain him. Don't use the same force on a child who is acting out as you would on an adult attacker.

In the ancient Biblical writings, the Greeks used two primary words that are translated as *anger*.

*Thumos* is a violent and passionate anger, which strikes suddenly and is just as quickly gone. To the ancients, it was like putting a match to a small amount of very dry straw. There is a quick flare up and it burns out just as quickly, with no lingering residue. It does not set the entire forest on fire.

*Orga* is indignation, which gradually rises, and becomes settled deep inside the person. It becomes the person's natural disposition. It is slow burning, smoldering, and refuses to be pacified. This type of anger turns to bitterness and the person's heart becomes stone cold.

A well-known historical use of anger was when Jesus cleansed the temple of those who were cheating the people and corrupting the temple. His anger was *thumos*. It was quick, focused on the offender's actions but not destructive of people, and over quickly.

Saint Paul, the writer of much of the New Testament, said, "In you anger, do not sin." This was his way of saying be angry at injustice but do not be destructive. When you see a child being abused, you should become angry and step forward to protect the child.

He also said, "Do not let the sun go down while you are still angry." This was his way of saying "deal with it immediately" — while you know what or with whom you are angry. Deal with it before bedtime. Do not let the anger destroy your sleep or settle into you and become bitterness.

Your mother probably said, "Don't go to bed angry." She was right. We need to heed her admonition and not go to bed angry, at a child, partner, or anyone, as it will be much more difficult to resolve the anger in the morning. Anger grows wildly overnight, like a forest fire in the dry summer, and by morning can be unmanageable. Then we become masters at finding excuses for not dealing with it.

Focus your anger on the source of the anger. We all know situations in which a father became angry at his boss at work, got into road rage on the way home, and upon entering the home, ignores his wife, yells at the kids, and kicks the cat. Hence, the wife, the kids, and the cat say to themselves, "What did I do to deserve this?" Soon the entire house is filled with anger and fighting.

### Guidelines for Managing the Anger Monkey

**1:** Admit you are angry. For some, admitting to anger is very difficult because you don't want to see yourself as an angry person. Very few people will readily admit they are angry because we all want to see ourselves and have others see us in the most positive light. If you are still having difficulty admitting you are angry or identifying how you express it go, back to chapter five and review the section on the Anger Monkey.

**2:** Identify with whom or what you are angry. State it clearly to a safe person or write it down. Another good way that can be useful to adults and children is to draw a picture of the anger so you can see it. It is amazing what you might see. If you are going to draw a picture, be certain to have a variety of colored writing instruments, so you can see your rage in all its glory. Remember the common adage about "seeing red."

**3:** Resolve it quickly. Speak to the person and apologize. Even if you were not the worst offender in the disagreement, you probably had some part in it.

**4:** Forgive the one who has offended you. We will go into more detail on forgiveness in chapter eight.

**5:** Do something physical. When you are in the grip of anger, you are going through a massive physical and emotional transformation. Your body is gearing up for the classical fight or flight response. It is amazing how dumb we become when we are angry. We can't think or talk clearly. This is because as we become angrier the blood drains away from our brain. Clearly, anger has a physical component. We need to quickly work it out of our body or it will do considerable damage to us. Mow the grass. Go for a jog. Play ball with the kids.

**6:** Lower your expectations of others. Most of us have higher expectations of others than we do of ourselves. We get angry with others for things that we give ourselves permission to do. Expect from others what you expect of yourself. Maybe even expect less of them than yourself. It is not fair to hold others to standards we do not have for ourselves. Much of your anger is the disparity between what someone has done to you and what you expected from him. The higher your expectations, the more frequently you are at risk at becoming angry.

**7:** Resolve that you will identify and resolve your anger more quickly the next time.

The issue isn't whether or not you ever have to wrestle with the anger monkey. The question is, will it control you or will you control it, to your advantage?

*Managing Your Guilt Monkey*

Is this your number one monkey? More women than men seem to have this one. Women often wonder why men seem less moved by guilt and they often get frustrated when it does not work on the men in their lives. It seems many women conclude that if a man cannot be moved to express guilt, then he cannot be trusted.

I have a theory that men are less moved by guilt than the women in their lives because it is a re-creation of what their mothers tried to do to them. This is not an attempt to blame mothers for all their sons' problems. Just watch other mothers, or yourself, when disciplining boys and girls.

Typically, the same tactics are used on both. Girls seem to respond more to the guilt messages while boys soon learn to shut them out. Little boys seem to shut out the guilt messages and stand compliantly listening until she is done. Then they walk away with less guilt sensitivity than when the lecture or request to apologize began. Now they are more skilled than before at blocking out the female voice and her demands. Adult women wonder why it seems their men never really listen to them, but it can be traced to early childhood.

Here is the dilemma for little boys. Much of the disciplining falls to mothers, because typically mothers have more time with the children and are more inclined to see the inappropriate behavior or want to address it. Fathers can be too good at letting things pass.

When mother starts to correct or lecture a little boy:

- What happens to him?
- What are his options?

He is not permitted to kick, hit, scream, or talk back to his mother. The times he tried to talk back, he quickly concluded he could not outtalk mother. When he dared to hit her, he quickly discovered she was more powerful, and he lost the contest. The only option left is to stand there, pretend he is listening, repeat what she wants to hear, and get it over with as soon as possible so he can go back to playing. When he repeats the words she insists upon, he has his fingers crossed.

After a few times, he becomes a master at blocking out a woman's voice, while pretending to be listening. This principle can be illustrated with a ubiquitous Little Johnny tale: when he misbehaved, the schoolteacher insisted that Little Johnny go stand in the corner. He resisted because he wanted to stay in his seat. She insisted. Finally, when he was standing in the corner he could be heard to say, "I may be standing up on the outside but I am sitting down on the inside." Again, the sense of guilt is minimized.

When a woman puts on the mother or teacher tone, her mate is very likely to internally block her voice, guilt, and demands. The more she tries to get through, the more he will block. Don't forget, he has had years of practice, has honed the skill, and often does not even know he has shut down. In his mind, he is already moving on to "play." He is better at this interchange than she is, so she ends up going away angry and frustrated.

Guilt is a very interesting emotion. For some unfounded reason we believe everyone has the same type and degree of guilt as we do and they will be moved as we are.

As parents, we do need to instill some guilt and behavioral responsibility in our children; otherwise, they will not have a moral compass to guide them. There is a very fine line between stunting and developing healthy guilt in children.

We all need the guilt monkey, who will keep us on a higher moral plain. However, we cannot allow it to dominate our lives or we will live a miserable, guilt-ridden existence.

The guiding principle for adults is: listen to your guilt monkey. Then cognitively evaluate right and wrong based on the question, "Will it hurt others or me if I commit this act?"

*Managing Your Inadequacy Monkey*

The inadequacy monkey will keep you from being overly confident in taking risks, being boastful, or becoming a know-it-all. Admitting that you do not know how to do something may keep you alive and protect you from arrogance.

On the other hand, you must not allow the inadequacy monkey to control you or you will live a life of insecurity and underachievement.

One of the traits I see in people who have a keen sense of inadequacy is overcompensation. To cover up their feeling of inferiority, they exaggerate their skills and abilities. One young man I know who wears his hat cocked to the side and has a carefully perfected walk said, "You have to develop your walk so you can walk with an attitude." He has so perfected his walk and facial expression that it is extreme and he comes across as an actor. When we discussed his deep feeling of inadequacy he did everything he could to deny it and manipulate the conversation away from the topic. He knew that I could see that his act was a cover for his inadequacy.

Don't be fooled. When someone comes across as a phony, most likely they have a deep problem with inferiority and are trying hard to cover it.

When I conduct personality assessments, it is easy to detect this. Of course, if I confront a person on it he will hold to his position of superiority. One day I said to a candidate, "So your attention and concentration ability is greater than most highly successful professional athletes." Realizing he had been found out in his attempt to present himself as a superior person, he quickly started to backtrack.

The interesting thing about most people who feel inadequate is that usually they really are quite capable. Sometimes they *are* superior. The young man I just referred to is very bright. The feeling of inadequacy is a real feeling, but usually it is an incorrect feeling.

Sometimes a person uses the sense of inadequacy as a motivator to become a high achiever. Eventually he will crash if his exterior personality is build on a weak foundation of inadequacy. Over the past few years, we have seen several public and business leaders who were highly recognized for their achievements go to prison. I suspect that if we could look deeply inside many of them, we would see an inadequacy or inferiority monkey lurking in the corner of their mind, controlling them.

An executive in the financial world who had a strong record of accomplishment came to me for a comprehensive competency-based evaluation. He told me he believed he was a phony and his achievements were just luck. Upon completion of the evaluation, I informed him that he had superior intellectual abilities and that he should put away his self-doubt and trust himself and his ability. Over the next few years, he soared in his achievements and became a recognized leader in the financial sector in Canada.

A woman in Toronto, Canada, came and requested the same evaluation. She thought she was average, and was going to apply for a middle management position in a bank. I clearly remember saying, "You have all excellent skills and abilities necessary to do whatever you want *in retail*." I gave her some career research homework. Soon, she opened the first retail store of a US-based company in Ontario and was wildly successful. A few years later, she was recruited to become the president and CEO one of Canada's most visible companies. After a few years in that position she commented, "I never knew I could be so successful, make so much money, and have so much fun." She just needed to get the inadequacy monkey off her back.

Just like anger, fear, or guilt, there is a fine balance between listening to your monkey and letting it control and dominate your life.

If you want to feel *inferior*, compare yourself to five people who are excellent at a particular skill, and believe you should be equal to or superior to all of them. I guarantee you will soon feel inferior or inadequate.

If you want to feel good about yourself:

- Always try to be your best.
- Always strive to improve.
- Learn from your failures.

Remember, you do not always have to be *the* best—just do *your* best.

# Chapter 7: The Joy of Pain

Great joy and peace can come from great suffering. Great maturity only comes with great suffering.

When you are in emotional pain, it is the worst of times, but has the potential to be the best of times.

Hundreds of times, I have said to a person who was suffering from a great loss or betrayal or abandonment or physical anguish that he would look back on this time and see it as one of the most meaningful times in his life, *if* he worked through the pain and did not curse or deny it. Obviously, at that moment each of them thought I was a bit strange for rejoicing in their pain.

Pain gets our attention like nothing else. We are masters at focusing on our empty activities and possessions we have in front of us.

In our North American society, we have this strange but universal view that pain and suffering are bad. We also tend to conclude that if we are experiencing this agony then we must be bad. Therefore, we want to rid ourselves of this pain, immediately or sooner. This is not to say that pain in and of itself is good. We do need to understand that only in pain and suffering, if properly viewed, can we be led to a deeper understanding of ourselves, our purpose, and our world.

Pain and suffering force us to address life's three most critical questions:

- Who am I?
- What am I doing here (on this earth)?
- Who are they (i.e., others)?

Not until you are ready and able to answers these questions are you ready to begin living and ready to be content with the reality of your death. We are not prepared to fully live until we are prepared to die.

The divas that run around the world going from party to party, from shopping spree to shopping spree, from one illicit affair to another, always trying to get media attention by doing shocking things with no sense of responsibility and no meaningful purpose are, of all people, *not* to be admired and emulated. They are, of all people, most miserable, even if they do not know it or admit it.

The most miserable people are those who are so out of touch with themselves and life that they do not even know they are miserable. Eventually you will have to come face to face with yourself and the real purpose of life or you will self-destruct.

If you will work through your emotional pain and come out the other side, you will always come out a more spiritual person than when you went in.

We need pain and suffering to force us to face our spiritual side, our spiritual needs, and who we are on the deepest level. We need pain and suffering to get us to see that there is more to life than the physical things we collect and the relationships we take so lightly.

The bumper sticker that says "He who dies with the most toys wins" is absolutely not true. These individuals are only trying to find some meaning in their empty lives.

Who really dies the most fulfilled and with fewest regrets—the one with the most toys or the one with the deepest level of spirituality that is manifested in his daily life, in how he lives and treat others? Is the winner the one with the most toys or the one with the purest heart? Is it the one with the boats, ATVs, sports cars, or Mother Theresa? The one who dies the most satisfied has lived the most satisfying life.

Even if you claim you are not a spiritual person and do not believe in God or a spiritual being, and therefore have no need for pain and suffering, I believe you need pain and suffering more than anyone. It will get your attention, so you will come to see the deeper and more significant things in life and cease to focus on your selfish self.

Leo Tolstoy, the philosopher (don't dismiss him as a theologian), says,

> The essence of any religion lies solely in the answer to the question: why do I exist, and what is my relationship to the infinite universe that surrounds me? It is as impossible for there to be a person with no religion (i.e., without any kind of relationship to the world) as it is for there to be a person without a heart. He may not know that he has a religion, just as a person many not know that he has a heart, but it is no more possible for a person to exist without religion than without a heart.[14]

As human beings, we are the most unique among all living creatures. We not only experience pain and suffering, we are intellectually capable of evaluating it and learning from it. Even though we are capable of learning from our pain, not everyone chooses to learn.

God is not some sadistic person who receives great joy from seeing His creation suffer. However, sometimes He has to take a big stick to get our attention. It is in the personal tragedies that one looks inward and seeks solace from prayer and religious services. Sadly, too often it takes the premature death of a loved one, a Hurricane Katrina, or a massacre at Virginia Tech. Suddenly people pray who have not prayed in years and the university campus is now open to displays of Christianity and transforms into a place where thousands pray together openly on the drill field.

C. S. Lewis wrote:

> Everyone has noticed how hard it is to turn our thoughts to God when everything is going well with us. We "have all we want" is a terrible saying when "all" does not include God. We find God an interruption. As St. Augustine says somewhere, God wants to give us something, but cannot, because our hands are full—there's nowhere for him to put it.[15]

When one is suffering and cannot find God or purpose in the suffering, the common question raised is, "If there is a God, why is He silent and not answering my prayers?" The answer, as a good friend recently said, is "Faith is born when we drink the cup of suffering and silence."

Suffering is one thing—but suffering and not immediately getting an answer is entirely different. People go for years with little acknowledgement of their spirituality and when disaster strikes expect that they should immediately receive a special vocal message from God in answer to their prayers. What right do they have to even expect an answer after you have for years ignored, or, at best, given token acknowledgement to the Almighty?

Do you think He is some kind of a slot machine where you put a quarter in, turn the handle, and get the answer you want? Most likely He is responding to you. You just do not like the answer, so you say "Where is He?" or "He has not answered my prayer." Or are you such strangers that you would not recognize His voice even if He did speak to you?

A review of the saints of the Old Testament of the Bible quickly reveals that all the men and women we admire suffered greatly and often had a long wait for their answer from God. The list is lengthy.

There is David, who went from being the boy hero by killing a giant to being hunted down by the king he honored and protected. Read his Psalms and relate to his moods that range from rejoicing to despair, from praising God to wondering if He was there or cared. One of the common denominators for those who suffered was they never received the answer as quickly as they wanted, nor did it come in the form they expected.

You, too, must learn that sometimes you are not in charge of the timing—how long you will suffer or *how* you will suffer. However, there are times when you are in charge of how long you will suffer.

When you chose to hold on to resentments, destructive anger, debilitating guilt, or immobilizing fear, you are deciding how long you will suffer. When you chose to hold on to the pain, you are holding on to it because you are getting something out of it.

Maybe you feel the need to be a victim, or pitied or protected by your emotion. Maybe you need to keep this old destructive thought or feeling because you believe you have a right to keep it. Or possibly you are afraid to find out who you really are without this emotional burden.

We have a thousand ways to put off examining our souls and looking at our spirituality. We allow everything else to fill our day and crowd our lives with meaningless thoughts and behaviors. Nevertheless, when emotional pain afflicts us or immobilizes us, it demands to be attended to *now*, if not sooner.

Pain will not stand in line and wait its turn.

It cannot be satisfied with recreation or work.

You cannot put off forever dealing with your soul. C. S. Lewis wrote, "God whispers to us in our pleasures, speaks to us in our conscience, but shouts in our pains: it is His megaphone to rouse a deaf world."[16]

Do you have a tin ear or are you willing to listen when pain overtakes you? Why not listen and learn long before you have the pain so you can use your spiritual strength to get you through the emotional pain? Can you imagine a fire department waiting to examine the fire before firefighters are trained or equipment is purchased? No, when you need them, you want them to be ready for any situation. So explain to yourself why you will wait until a crisis to discover if you have the spiritual reserves ready for the pain. It is not a question of *if* you will need the reserves, but *when*.

When the emotional pain strikes, do not curse it. As painful and horrible as it can be make friends with it (i.e. explore it), try to understand it, learn from it, and change your behavior if necessary. When pain strikes, stop and listen. When the pain stops do not automatically rejoice, because the secession of your emotional pain may not be a good sign for you.

"Tribulations cannot cease until God either sees us remade or sees that our remaking is hopeless."[17] Maybe your pain has stopped because you were not ready or willing to learn your lesson.

It is quite interesting to look at Biblical, historical, or contemporary examples of people who have had many emotional hurts and challenges. Some have risen to the same challenge time and time again. You admire them and say, "I don't think I could have handled it as well as he did." You admire the person who emerged from the challenge. Behind almost every great moral, spiritual, and mature achiever you meet, you will find an amazing story of overcoming or continuous coping.

It seems with each hurt these people grow stronger and deeper. It is almost as if God is saying, "Now you have chosen to pass the test. I have given you a little rest to enjoy the emotional and spiritual growth you have made. Now I am going to give you the opportunity to grow more, to discover more of yourself."

To others, it appears God is saying, "You failed the previous opportunity I have given you. You have not taken advantage of it to learn and grow. Now I am going to give you another opportunity to find the real you so you can reach a new spiritual and emotional depth."

Think of the Old Testament story about the children of Israel wandering around in the desert for forty years. When you look on a map and track their course, you will quickly learn that if they had walked in a straight line they could have completed the journey in eleven days. It took them forty years to learn the lessons God was trying to teach them.

Don't be too critical. You and I are probably no better at learning the lessons God wants us to learn. That is why He keeps bringing up the same issues again and again in your life. Not until you have learned the first lesson will He take you on to the second.

Look at the people you know! Who has a sense of peace and purpose because he has experienced great pain and chosen to work through it rather than curse it, God, and the world?

Take a close look at yourself and ask yourself, "Where am I in my emotional and spiritual growth? Am I a better person or a bitter person?"

Which person am I?

- Have I cursed the hurt and failed to learn?
- Have I learned from the previous hurts and grown?
- Is God giving me another opportunity to grow?

As a therapist, it never ceases to amaze me that after I've helped someone work through his hurt of abuse, abandonment, loss, depression, marital breakdown, addiction, or whatever challenge he had to face, he invariably finds a level of spirituality he had never previously experienced. Yet it was not our objective to work on his spirituality.

However, as a person grows emotionally, it appears he is now free to explore and experience a new spiritual depth— then he is amazed to look around and see that others do not understand him. Once you have climbed Mount Everest and try to explain the experience, the only ones who can grasp what you are talking about are the ones who have been there.

When you find someone who has had a similar hurt and overcome it, it is as if you have a deep understanding of each other. This person becomes your soul mate. By some unknown deep level of intuition, we find ourselves drawn to persons who have had similar experiences and found healing.

It is also true that bitter people are attracted to bitter people. They spend their time commiserating with each other. Overcomers do not enjoy spending time with the bitter. We tend to move away from them to avoid being contaminated by their negativism.

Much of the Christianity that is being taught today is as guilty of trying to avoid learning the hard lessons as the world at large. Many churches are teaching that if you have the right degree of faith, your problems will disappear, or you will be healed, or whatever. Others are teaching a prosperity religion—that if you have faith, you will never have needs or poverty.

But with this type of Christianity, when the problems do not disappear instantly, the believer feels he lacks faith and feels defeated. People who teach the type of religion that immediately solves all problems are just laying another heavy burden on those who are already struggling with marriages, addictions, finances, or health.

Jesus Christ never taught that faith would bring you instant release of your burden, that you would easily overcome your temptation, addiction, or whatever. He very clearly stated, "If I go away I will send you the Comforter." Other translations use the word "Counselor," "Helper," or "Holy Spirit." Jesus went on to say His Comforter would be with you and in you.

(We are referring to the Holy Spirit, Comforter, or Counselor as "He" because in the original Greek text these terms are in the masculine tense, not the neuter. The Helper is a spiritual being, not an it or a thing.)

Jesus did not say He would send a Healer who would instantly take away all your physical and emotional pain. He did not say He would send a benefactor who would pay all your bills. He did not say He would send a guardian angel that would always protect you from harm.

Jesus said He would send a Comforter, Companion, Buddy, and Encourager. The point is simple and profound. He knew we would continuously experience hurt, pain, distress, confusion, hatred, rejection, poverty, abuse, fear, disease, war, famine, and so on in this world.

He wanted to leave us with a Helper. The function of the Holy Spirit of God is *to help* us through the tough times, *not to rescue* us from tough times. The function of the Holy Spirit, the Comforter, is to encourage us *while* we are afraid so that in the midst of tragedy disease, war, and threats of all kinds we would never be alone.

His mission is to stick closer than a brother so no matter what is threatening or happening to us, we can have peace in our souls while in a world of confusion, turmoil, and pain.

When Jesus was here on this earth, He chose to be limited by time and space. The great news is that in sending us the

Comforter, He is not limited by time or space. He can be with you all the time no matter where you are.

- If you are in the depths of the sea, He is there.
- If you are on the moon, He is there.
- If you are alone dying in the hospital bed, He is there.
- If you are alone on your bed, in the middle of the night, in great distress, He is there.
- If you need someone to tell your deepest secret to, He is there to listen. And He doesn't condemn or gossip.

The Holy Spirit of God is like the wind. He is everywhere all the time. You cannot see the wind, or Him, but you can feel the wind, see the motion, and experience the results.

Forget the notion that you will be insulated from pain and hurt if you are a believer. Accept the ever-present Friend, Comforter, Buddy, and Companion. Get acquainted with Him today so you will be friends *before* the crisis strikes.

You may not feel Him, but He is there, if you will call and listen. Spend more time listening than talking. Only one person can talk at a time.

The Comforter is also a Counselor. It is His job to convict us of our destructive thoughts and behaviors in order for us to change and have peace of heart, soul, and mind. It is His job to give you assurance and peace when you have said and done the right thing. He gives you the good feeling that comes over you after you have helped a friend, fed the sick, protected or helped a child, said kind words of encouragement, or let someone into the traffic ahead of you.

The tragedy of spirituality is that we have access to all the help we need, yet we fail to ask Him to help us or readily thank Him when He does. It is as if we are starving to death while sitting at a table piled high with the best nutritious food possible, and we refuse to eat because we do not believe it is real.

Pascal said, "We are created with an inner vacuum which only God can fill." When you feel the pain in the vacuum of your heart, let God fill it with His Comforter.

Victor Frankel, a German psychiatrist and survivor of the Nazi concentration camps, wrote of his experiences and observations of the greatest struggle for survival in the history of humankind. *Man's Search for Meaning* and *The Unconscious God* are two of the greatest books ever written. If you will read them with an open spirit and mind, it will touch the depths of your soul. Frankel said, "Despair is suffering without purpose."[18] This is such an important concept that I believe you should memorize it.

The reason your suffering is so painful is you are unable to see the bigger picture—to see how suffering can help *you* become a more spiritual person. Forget about needing to understand why someone died or that there was yet another tragedy in the news.

I intend no disrespect for the dead, but the lesson is for the living, not the dead. Will you allow this or use this to transform you into a deeper being? You do not need the specific answer written in the sky if you will see the bigger picture—that this is another opportunity for you to examine your life and your purpose.

# Chapter 8:  Better or Bitter

Growth in wisdom may be exactly measured by decrease in bitterness.
—Friedrich Nietzsche, German philosopher (1844–1900)

M ost of the time you will not have the option to choose the hurt and pain you experience. However, you always have the freedom to choose how you will respond to the situation.

In each painful event in your life, you will choose to become either:

- A better person or a bitter person.
- A victorious person or a victim.

Whether or not you choose is *not* an option. This is an either/or situation. You will either choose life or death, freedom or bondage, better or bitter, victor or victim. There is no middle ground any more than there is the option to choose a little of each.

Let me emphasize one more time: there are only two options and you are the one making the choice. This is not a situation where you can say, "He made me do it." If you play the blame game then you have automatically chosen to be a victim and you are on the path to bitterness. It is always your choice as to whether or not the heat will temper you and make you stronger or melt you and destroy you.

Psychiatrists like Rollo May and others recognize that any moment can be responded to in one of two ways: "a blessing for growth or a curse that cripples."[19]

Will you choose to play the victim because it gives you an excuse for being irresponsible, angry, and bitter? Our world is saturated with self-declared victims. Our entire society seems to be screaming, "I am not responsible because my father was an alcoholic," or "my parents divorced," or "we were poor," or "I am a minority," or "I was bullied in school so this gives me the right to cheat, lie, be addicted, or kill someone."

And of course the media, many courts, and special interest groups are more than ready to label these people as victims and not hold them responsible for their behavior. While it may look like a great way to avoid responsibility, it is a sad commentary on those who accept it for choosing to participate in the victim game.

A great way to destroy any sense of self-esteem is to choose to play the victim role. Playing this role does nothing to help you become a better person. It just contributes to your sense of bitterness.

The other option is to choose to be victorious, to rise above the challenge, and feel good about overcoming a great obstacle. Then you will have bragging rights and a real story to share the next time you are in a group of overcomers. Besides, you will certainly feel better about yourself than when you were bragging about being a victim.

Which of the following has happened to you? Your baby died, your spouse betrayed you, your children neglected or deceived you, you developed an incurable illness, you became financially destitute, or your loved one was kidnapped or murdered. None of these, or any other painful situation, is easy to deal with. However, when it is placed at your doorstep, rise to the challenge and be better for it.

It is not what has happened to you that determines whether you will become better or bitter, victim or victor. In chapter four I described the man who was adopted and violently killed a young boy. However, there are many stories of persons who came from the same or more difficult backgrounds yet chose to make a contribution to society and not act out in violence.

Which will it be for you better or bitter, contributor or prisoner? The great preacher Harry Emerson Fosdick said, "Bitterness imprisons life; love releases it."

*Better Is Not The Absence Of Bitterness*

There is no such thing as a vacuum in your heart and soul. Your mind, heart, and soul are filled with something. As an adult, you get to choose what to keep and live by and what you want to discard. There seems to be a natural law that emptiness is automatically filled with negative feelings, thoughts, and behaviors. Remember your mother quoting the old adage, "Idle hands are the devil's workshop"! She knew if her children were not occupied with good things that they would quickly and automatically gravitate to mischievous things. Test the proposition by putting three little boys in a room with nothing to do. Do you think they will sit and plot how they could help their mother with the housework, or be nice to their sister?

It is a fallacy to say that violence and sexual inappropriateness in the visual, music, or print media do not influence behavior. Show me a violent or corrupt person who never watched or enjoyed such material! It is, plain and simple, "garbage in, garbage out." You are either going to fill yourself with positive material that produces positive thoughts and behavior, or you are going to fill yourself with destructive material that will produce destructive behavior.

You know that if you eat tainted food you will get ill from food poisoning. Why are we so distorted in our thinking to believe that a person can put abuse of others and violence into his system and expect to become a kind, generous person? You lie in bed at night and watch the late news, which is filled with crime and violence, and wonder why you have trouble sleeping. Turn it off. Read something peaceful and tranquil or listen to quiet, soothing music. We think we can get away with polluting our minds and it will have no affect on us—but that's simply not the case.

*Your Philosophy of Life Determines Your Response*

It is not the event in your life or the degree of pain it brings that determines your better or bitter response. You will make your response decision long before the pain comes. Your choice comes from your philosophy of life.

- If you believe only good things should happen to you because you are a good person, when pain comes, it is likely you will become bitter.
- If you believe pain and suffering is unfair, you will likely become bitter when the pain hits.
- If you believe bad things only happen to other people, you will likely become bitter when it is your turn for pain.
- If you believe you have already had your share of pain, then you will likely become bitter.

- If you have not built a support system of family and friends, you will likely become bitter.
- If you believe you are exceptional and others should always give to you and protect you, you will likely become bitter.
- If you believe you always deserve the best, you will likely become bitter.
- If you believe that God should immediately come to your rescue and remove your pain, you will likely become bitter.

*or*

- If you believe pain and suffering are a normal course of life, you will likely grow through the pain.
- If you believe in yourself and your ability, you will likely grow through pain.
- If you have built a support network, you will have the external resources to help you through the pain.
- If you believe in a loving God who is concerned about you, and you appropriate His Spirit, the Comforter, you will likely grow through the pain.

## Choosing Bitterness

Choosing bitterness does not reverse the tragedy, cure it, or make the pain go away. It only intensifies the pain and makes it last longer.

Who have you chosen to become bitter at—yourself, others, or God? How has this helped you through the hurt and pain? If you are honest, you will admit it has not helped. Are you still bitter over your ex-spouse? Please explain to me why you want to continue hurt yourself and destroy your happiness over someone you don't even like! Why are you allowing the person who hurt you continue to control your life? Does this make sense?

Bitterness is a cancer. It eats away at you until you are emotionally and physically ill. It kills your body and soul. The cure may need to be radical and painful. That is why most people prefer to keep the bitterness. I heard a woman say the best time of her life was when she was going through cancer treatment, because it was the only time in her life when others genuinely cared for her. This is both tragic and refreshing. Tragic in that her life before had been lonely. Refreshing, because there are people who really care for the hurting.

*The Benefits of Bitterness*

- Loneliness: No one will bother with you.
- Friendless: You will not have to give to anyone.
- Poor Health: Bitterness is a key contributor to poor mental and physical health. It increases the likelihood of strokes, high blood pressure, and much more. Of course, you will have more trips to the doctor to get his sympathy.
- Hopeless: You do not need to worry about bad things happening because you already know they will.
- Cheerless/Joyless: Life is void of the awful noise of laughter.
- Purposeless: You have nothing to work toward, you only need to do the bare essentials.
- Conflict: You will see everyone as an adversary and hurt them before they can hurt you.
- More Bitterness: Oh goodie, now I can be more miserable and have more anger power.

*The Benefits of Choosing Better*

Now here is a no-brainer! If you chose to overcome pain, and grow from and through the terrible event, here is what you will get: more friends, peace of mind, respect, purpose of life, less conflict, better physical and mental health, more joy and laughter, and the knowledge that you've made a positive contribution to society.

If you want to live the better life, then you will seek to become all you can so you can happily give to others. Better is not the absence of bitterness. Better is when one is free of bitterness and happily giving and helping others.

The key components of a well-balanced life are:

- A sense of purpose
- Love and intimacy
- Development of your spirituality
- Friendship
- Meaningful work
- Time for recreation

Now compare the bitterness choice with the better choice. Why are you holding yourself back from seeking the better way? Chose it and begin today. You cannot lose.

Several years ago the book *I'm OK, You're OK*, based on transactional analysis, was very popular. The concept prompted choosing a lifestyle of the title over the less healthy styles of the other possibilities, that is, "I'm Not OK, You're Not OK" or "I'm OK, You're Not OK."

Karen Horney, a well-respected psychologist popularized the three life positions we can take:

1. Moving toward people
2. Moving away from people
3. Moving against people

Which of these life-style positions have you chosen?

Abraham Maslow, discussed the personal internal conflict of whether to grow or seek safety in his *Toward a Psychology of Being:*

> Every human being has both sets of forces within him. One set clings to safety and defensiveness out of fear, tending to regress backward, hanging on to the past, afraid to grow ... the other set of forces impels him forward toward wholeness of Self and uniqueness of Self, toward full functioning of all his capabilities, toward confidence in face of the external world. (16)

The question for you is, which force will you chose for your life?

# Chapter 9: Healing the Hole in Your Heart

Forgiveness is a must in any family problem where there has been deep hurt, betrayal, or disloyalty. If there can be no reconciliation, forgiveness is the process that enables the forgiver to get on with his or her life unencumbered with the pain of betrayal.
—P. W. Coleman[21]

G ood news! There is hope!
Even though you have emotional pain from the deficit in your heart, which others did not properly fill, you can take charge and bring healing to yourself. You do not need to live with the pain; you do not need to seek destructive ways to try to manage the hurt.

It is important to understand that once there is a hole in your heart, it cannot be completely healed. You will always have some sense of emptiness, but you can use constructive means to alleviate the pain. When you have a headache and take an aspirin to lessen the discomfort, this does not mean you will never have another headache. It means you know how to quickly and constructively reduce the pain each time the symptoms arise.

Webster's Dictionary defines healing as "to make whole, to restore to health, to cause an undesirable condition to be overcome."[22] Since your heart was not whole to begin with, it cannot be made whole again. However, you can take control—you can cause an undesirable condition to be overcome.

After a perpetrator has been convicted of a horrible murder, you might see an insensitive news interviewer ask the family if they now have "closure." When I hear this, I want to speak out to the interviewer—don't you know the family of the murdered person will never experience closure? The best they can hope for is to find some peace in their hearts and learn how to cope and live with the pain. Events like birthdays, the anniversary of the death, and visual reminders will suddenly resurrect the pain in the heart. The scab of the wound will be torn off again and again and the healing will have to begin again and again.

However, there is hope. Once you learn how to overcome the pain, you can use the healing method as needed. Though the hole in your heart can never be—once and for all—completely healed, there are things you can do to minimize your pain. You can take action and bring the pain quickly under control each time it reemerges. As you do this, you will become more and more effective in managing and minimizing the pain.

If you believe you have completely gotten over a major hurt or pain, you are probably only fooling yourself. For example, there is no such thing as complete healing for the victim of child abuse, the death of a child, abandonment, or other types of violence that were perpetrated on you. Just as physical violence leaves marks on your body, so does emotional violence leave scars on your heart and soul. The pain may be manifested in many different ways. Some expressions of pain are very unhealthy and others appear to be healthy.

My interest was piqued by a television documentary on a family in England who had fifteen children and planned for more. The quest for more children was primarily the mother's idea, though the father was an excellent father. One of their adult children commented that he did not know what his mother was going to do when she could no longer have children. As I watched, I kept wondering why she was so possessed with the idea of having as many children as possible. Finally, the reason emerged. The mother said she was born to a single mother who often left her alone for long periods of time—even when she was as young as three. The little girl decided that she never again wanted to experience the pain of being left alone, nor did she want her children to experience the pain of being alone. In this case, there is nothing destructive with how this woman is attempting to fill the hole in her heart. However, it is unfortunate that she has not had help in healing the hole in her heart rather than feeling the constant need to overcome the fear of loneliness by having more children.

There are hundreds of destructive ways one can choose to cope with the pain in his heart. We addressed some of these in chapter four (Meeting Your Monkeys). Other destructive ways include, anger, bitterness, addictions (including drugs, food, shopping, sex) blaming others, self-blame, depression, and destructive relationships. Sigmund Freud labeled many of these destructive ways ego defense mechanisms. They are mental processes that a person uses to control his anxiety and pain. They include:

- Denial: Arguing against an anxiety-provoking stimuli by stating it doesn't exist.

- Displacement: Taking out your emotions on a less threatening target, like hitting a child in place of an adult because, they can't fight back.
- Intellectualization: Avoiding an unacceptable emotion by focusing on intellectual pursuits.
- Projection: Accusing others of the habits you have.
- Rationalization: Supplying a logical or rational reason as opposed to the real reason.
- Repression or Suppression: Pushing it into the unconscious.

You would not put arsenic on your open sore, so why chose destructive methods to try and heal an aching heart?

*Healthy Ways to Bring Healing To The Hole In Your Heart*

1. Acknowledge you have a hole in your heart.

The hole in your heart may be small or large, but I am certain you have one. Maybe you missed the joy of having siblings with whom you could play and fight. Maybe you never had the thrill of having grandparents who were close to you and gave you the unconditional grandparent love. You may have been raised in a great single parent family, but perhaps there was much you did not get, because the other parent was nonexistent.

The challenge is to be willing to look into your past, take off the rose-colored glasses, and see your family for what it really was and is. Don't just look for "bad" things. Also, look for "good" things you missed out on. Many people resist looking back; they say "My parents and family were like most other people's" (implying "we were normal)," or "I don't want to blame my parents." But this is not about blaming your parents. I don't believe in blaming. Blaming is counterproductive. This is about having the courage to see your family for what it was in order to learn about yourself.

Saying, "I don't want to blame my family" is a cop-out for refusing to take a serious look at yourself. Like it or not, you are the product of your family.

Typically, that which you dislike in others or dislike about your family is that which you dislike the most about yourself, or vow you never want to be. However, you are very susceptible to becoming that—if you are not already showing signs of it. The child raised in an alcoholic or abusive family vows he will never be like his birth family. Yet it is clear that many children of alcoholic or abusive families become like their parents.

When you honestly look back, you will find some deficiencies. First, take a candid look at your parent's deficiencies. Then look deeper at their parents, your grandparents. You will likely see a generational pattern. I never cease to be amazed at how many adults know little or nothing about their grandparents. Doesn't the absence of knowledge of one's grandparents speak volumes? Why all the silence? If they were great, you would have interacted with them or heard about them and your parents would speak proudly about them.

I have had the pleasure of pushing many people to closely examine their parents and grandparents. When they look beyond their parents and learn about their grandparents' life, they usually see a pattern. My clients have discovered their parent or grandparent was put into a foster home, or there was physical or sexual abuse, alcohol, poverty, death or murder, or they became the adult to their parents or siblings, or one sibling was chosen over the others as the favorite, or love was conditional upon performance. When the truth is discovered, it is amazing how quickly my client's anger turned to sadness or acceptance of his parent. You, too, can have that transformation. Remember—the truth will set you free.

After not having any contact with my father for most of my adolescent and teen years, I was determined to see who he was. Full of anger toward him, at age nineteen I went to Miami, Florida, and, without forewarning him, I knocked on his front door one Sunday morning. When he answered he said, "Who are you and what do you want?" After I'd introduced myself, he invited me in to stay for a few days. When I left, all my anger was gone. I thought to myself as I went away, "Thank you, God. I am glad he left. Life would have been worse if he had not left."

From my personal experience and my many years as a therapist, I am convinced when we see our family members for what they really were/are, we will find release from much of our pain. But you must have the courage to face them before you can find release. You will not find yourself until you are willing to objectively see your family of origin. Like it or not, you are the product of your family.

Now, do you still want to hold to the position that there are no deficiencies in your family history? Are you still holding on to the myth of your perfect family? Do you still want to hold to the family lie that "we were normal"? Then why do you have deficiencies and emotional pain? If you have the courage to trace the roots of your pain, where do they go? Certainly not to someone you never knew.

If you still have difficulty acknowledging that you have some work to do on yourself, maybe you need to look at your symptoms first, and then trace backwards to the source.

2. Identify precisely the deficiencies in your past life.

Now that you have acknowledged you are willing to take a look at your past, it is time to be specific. Look for the good times and the good memories and review them, as well as the painful times and deficiencies.

If you have not already started, now is the time to begin writing in your personal daily journal. It is time to begin writing about your past. This writing and reviewing of what you have written from your discoveries needs to become a lifetime habit. You may say you don't have time, but did you know that President Ronald Regan handwrote in his personal diary for many years, including every night of his presidency?

3. Stop blaming others.

Blaming others says more about you than them. It says you don't want to accept responsibility for your life. It says you prefer to live a life of bitterness. If you have not dropped the blame game by now, go back and reread chapter eight (Better or Bitter).

4. Give up the pity party and the poor-me games.

If you want to stay depressed and unhappy, keep up the pity party. Because if you give this stuff up, your life will change. Give up the blame, grow up, and you will be amazed at how much better life can be. Life will be better, not bitter.

Previously we have discussed that we keep our emotions for a purpose. So what are you getting out of your pain?

- Does your anger make you feel more powerful and less vulnerable?
- Does your depression get you attention and pity?
- Does telling your sad story get you attention and provide an excuse for your present bad behavior?

Now, be honest and pencil in why you are keeping your pain: _____
_____.

5. Discover how the hurt and pain has made you strong.

Why is it that when we have experienced emotional hurt and pain we automatically focus on how it has damaged us? It is true there is damage. However, have you ever considered that inherent in the hurt are the seeds that can make you strong, even outstanding? The history books and biographies are replete with the stories of persons who faced trials and turned lemons into lemonade. We look at the stories and admire these people. Now it is your turn to rise above the cruel circumstances that were dumped in your lap.

Have your circumstances…

- Made you more independent and self-sufficient?
- Prepared you for major challenges and struggles that came later?
- Made you more compassionate and empathic?
- Given you a life purpose?
- Made you a better mother or father because you were determined to overcome your past?
- Led you down a path of faith and spirituality?
- Impacted your career selection so that you now alleviate others' pain and suffering?
- Helped you to see and be prepared for the complexities of life?

6. Use the good emotions and memories from your other chambers to give you strength, joy, and healing.

While it is impossible for someone to fill a chamber in your heart that does not have his name on it, he can make a great contribution toward your emotional well-being. You must decide to focus on the good you *have* received.

- Stop focusing on what you did not get and focus on what you did receive.

- Stop focusing on the half-empty cup and focus on the half-full cup.
- Stop thinking everyone else had it better than you, and focus on others who had it much tougher.
- Stop thinking about how badly you had it and realize it could have been worse.

Be grateful for ... the excellent stepparent, grandparent, aunt, uncle, teacher, neighbor, best friend's parents, foster parent, or significant other who loved you and gave himself to you. These individuals gave to you because they *chose* to, not because it was expected of them, because they were not your parents.

Appropriating what you received from others to the healing of your pain is like transferring money from your savings account to your checking account. It was yours to begin with, now you can spend it to mitigate the pain.

7.  Choose to forgive.

The foundation stone to emotional healing is forgiveness. Your hurt and pain will never subside until you can genuinely forgive. Most mental health professionals see the value of forgiveness and encourage their clients to move in the direction of forgiveness.

The foundation of Christianity is forgiveness. You will not find a deep level of spirituality until you are able to forgive. Failure to forgive stunts your emotional and spiritual growth.

When you hate someone, you give him control over your life. Carrying resentment of him in your mind and soul keeps you awake at night, keeps you irritable in the daytime, keeps you from having a deep sense of peace and joy. It causes you to have high blood pressure and other physical ailments. You spend your money on lawyers trying to get even rather than on enjoyable vacations. The fact is, as long as you carry resentment and do not forgive, the resentment will always hurt you more than the offender.

*The most amazing thing to me about the refusal to forgive is that you allow the person you like the least to control your life.* Now does that make sense? Think about it: does it make sense to let the one you see as your adversary control your physical, emotional, and spiritual well-being, and keep you from having the joy of life?

Does it make sense to kick a skunk? Does it make sense to challenge a grisly bear empty-handed? The answer to these questions is obvious. So why isn't the decision to forgive obvious?

*Excuses For Not Forgiving*

I call these excuses, not reasons, because you are capable of forgiving the one who offended you. You are trying to justify your poor reasoning and absolve yourself of guilt for not forgiving. We both know this really does not work.

1. I am not ready to forgive and forget. The old admonishment to forgive and forget is neither wise nor possible. To forgive does not mean that you let your guard down so you can be hurt again. Forgiveness simply means you will give up your resentment and not your vigilance. If you know someone who sexually abused you when you were young and defenseless, you would be a fool to allow that person to spend time alone with your child. When President Ronald Regan negotiated a nuclear arms reductions treaty with Russia, his infamous statement was "trust but verify." When you forgive someone but you feel he is still untrustworthy, then don't trust him. However, neither do you need to hate him.

   It is not possible to forget. The mind is an amazing recording organ. It records and keeps all that it records. It is not possible to just say I will never remember that again. Interestingly, the more you concentrate on not remembering the more you remember.

2. The other person may not accept my forgiveness.

This is a cop-out. Your decision and ability to forgive is not predicated on the other person's response. If that were the case, if he died before you forgave him, you would be bound to resent him the remainder of your life. Does that seem fair or logical? A great many of the people I have seen who learned to forgive someone else were in situations where the one they hated was already dead. Sometimes they had been dead for years. Does it make sense for you to hate someone and let him control you long after he is six feet under? Forgive him! He can no longer hurt you. Let it go!

The fact is it's entirely possible that if you seek to forgive someone in person, he will not be willing to admit he's offended you at all. You should not let this person's denial or lack of cooperation stand in the way of your healing.

3. I have a right to continue to hate him.

Yes, you have the right to hate and resent anyone you want. Now don't you feel powerful and self-righteous? You also have the right to drink strychnine. It is hatred and unforgiveness that make suicide bombers and bomb builders who destroy innocent men, women, and children. Take a look at the cultural groups that hate each other and have been trying to destroy each other for centuries: they have not succeeded in destroying their perceived enemy. They *have* succeeded in destroying their own peace and tranquility of life. And they have succeeded in destroying the good life for their children and grandchildren. Your war may only consist of two people, but it is just as stupid and destructive.

4. I forgave him once but I keep resenting him.

This is what normally happens, because forgiveness is not a one-time event. You must make the decision to forgive and each time the feeling of resentment rears its ugly head you must say to yourself, "I chose to forgive (insert name) and I will continue to forgive him/her. I will not allow myself to be drawn back into resentment and hatred."

The best advice on this is to recall the person who asked Jesus, "Master, how often should I forgive my brother?" The reply was "seventy times seven." The point is not that you are to keep track and after he offends you 490 times you can get even. It means that you must keep on forgiving. You may have forgiven someone but ten years later a memory comes up and you have to forgive him again. Forgiveness is a continuous process. Each time you do it, it will become easier and easier.

5. I don't feel like it.

Of course you don't feel like it! You are angry, afraid, and you want to get even and protect yourself. If you wait until you *feel* like it you will probably never forgive. Forgiveness is a cognitive decision in which you choose to do what is best for yourself and the other person regardless of how you feel. Forgiveness is mind over feelings. You do many other things you don't feel like doing, like getting out of bed to go to work. You do it because it is best for your welfare. Refusal to forgive is a feeling. Forgiveness is an act of the will.

6. I don't know how.

This is a pathetic excuse if I ever heard one. I know that you have already forgiven many people for what they have done to you. If you have not, you are totally controlled by resentments you have chosen to keep. Forgiving is as simple as saying ten words: "I forgive (insert name) for what he has done to me."

7. I don't want to.

This is probably the most honest of all the excuses. Of course you do not want to. None of us ever wants to forgive. Somehow we believe that holding a grudge or hatred is easier than forgiving. We are proud people and forgiveness is a humbling act. Now, don't you feel good about yourself because you can behave as a six-year-old, hold your breath, have a little temper tantrum, and say, "I don't want to"?

9. I don't want to let him off the hook.

When you say this, you think you are controlling him. Wrong thinking! You are the one who is on the hook and not in control of your life. You are letting the one you hate control you. You have the assumption that as long as you hate him you are affecting his life. Wrong thinking again! Most likely he has long forgotten what happened. He has moved on with his life and you are still on the hook.

10. He has not asked for forgiveness.

Since when is your happiness and emotional peace and joy dependent on someone else's behavior? Since when is releasing your resentment dependent on some one else who may not even like you? Suppose he doesn't want to forgive you? Does this mean that you are now stuck for the rest of your life with a spirit of unforgiveness and you must live with bitterness in your heart? Of course not.

Healing the pain that is coming from the hole in your heart is completely in your hands. Will you choose wisdom, courage, and peace of mind—or stay in the pain of anger and resentment? Remember, it is your choice.

# Chapter 10:  The Generational Hole

We are the children of our past generations on both the paternal and maternal sides. We are not just the children of our birth parents. Nor are we self-contained entities who have been born and raised in an incubator with no outside influence. Far too many generations in our society have promoted the myth of individualism, which means we are solely the product of our own choices, and all we have to do is make up our minds to change and—abracadabra—we *are* changed.

I believe the quick-change artists and teachers who are teaching a false doctrine are doing a great injustice to all people challenged with making a change in their lives. They are heaping mountains of guilt on you for failing and discouraging you because you were not transformed in the blink of an eye. There is no such thing as developing a new habit in forty days that will last for a lifetime. You and I know it is not true. If it were true, one simple diet plan would have solved obesity and one self-help book would have made us all emotionally healthy.

The reason we admire people who have lost weight, stopped an addiction, or overcome depression, anger, shyness, or whatever is because we know how difficult it is to change. It is time to be honest. Change is difficult and painful, but not impossible. Many people have worked to change their lives and you can work on changing yours. You may not reach perfection, but you will be much further ahead of where you are now.

I hate exercise. A few years ago, I went to the gym four times a week for three years. When I stopped for a couple weeks, this so-called new lifetime habit was gone and I have not been back since. How many smokers do you know who were hospitalized for weeks with lung cancer were puffing again as soon as they were released? I dare you to give up your favorite daily fix of ice cream or chocolate (or whatever it is) for thirty days without a struggle and then not go back.

We are capable of change, but for any of us who have tried to make a significant change in our lives, we soon found out it was too difficult. Change is possible but rarely instantaneous or without massive struggle. The struggle of conquering something difficult is the best part. You feel much better about yourself and enjoy the taste of conquest when you have battled a giant and won. Listen to others who talk about overcoming. The happiest people are those who have had the greatest struggles. Our nature is that we do not get much thrill out of something that is easy.

The choices we make are critical to our development. However, we must never underestimate the impact of our family history. Often the choices we believe we are making freely are consistent with our historical family influence.

As I have stated previously, we are not blaming our parents. Rather, we need to understand our parents and grandparents so that we may understand ourselves.

As a therapist with over thirty years' experience, I constantly see shaped personalities or choices made as a direct connection to choices made by parents or grandparents or affected by tragic situations they experienced. A majority of therapists will agree that it is critical to understand your history in order to understand yourself and extricate yourself from the family pain.

Nor am I suggesting some form of predestination or fatalism, which teaches that we do not have a choice in who we are or what decisions we make. We are not saying all our lives were predetermined and the choices we make are not really our own. We are saying we are a combination of our past and our own uniqueness and decisions.

We are not just some spot in time; we are a living testimony to our family history. Of course, there are those exceptions who appear to have overcome a dysfunctional family system. Most of them will tell you it was a struggle—but worth it.

The hurt and pain your grandparents or great-grandparents experienced was commonly passed on to their children and grandchildren. The emotional pain you feel coming from the hole in your heart may actually be one or more generations old.

### An Illustration

A very unemotionally cold woman who did not know how to love and nurture left emptiness in her children's hearts. One of those children, who later became your mother, was very poor at loving and nurturing, which made it difficult for her to naturally love and nurture you. Now you wonder why you find it difficult to naturally be as warm and caring as you believe you should or would like to be. Or perhaps you don't think about it. You accept your parenting way as adequate so you pass the deficiencies on to your children. You don't know what happened to your grandparent or great-grandparent that caused her to become so cold and emotionally lacking.

The emotional emptiness you feel may be from your grandfather suddenly dying and leaving grandmother with several small children to raise. While she struggled with her grief, she found it impossible to love and nurture her children as she might have liked. The result is your mother growing up with a hole in her heart.

Possibly a grandparent or great-grandparent was an alcoholic. How did this affect their family and future generations? If you are struggling with an addiction, look at yourself and look backward to see if there is a family pattern.

Possibly grandfather was a closet pedophile who molested his children. Some in the family knew his behavior but no one confronted him or ever held him accountable. He passed on his destructive behavior to his sons or the pain of the abuse to his daughters. When therapists deal with sexually abused clients, one often finds a family history of abuse that has never been confronted.

Is there a long line of anger, abuse and destructiveness in your family? You may have to fight very hard to overcome this family tendency.

Do you have difficulty with intimacy? Who in your family was abandoned or abused, choosing to never again experience intimacy because it was too painful?

Is there a history of abandonment in your family? Where did it start? Are you at risk of perpetuating it? I have on occasion met people who felt compelled to leave their spouse and children. Even though they gave a feeble excuse, they really did not know why they felt so strongly to make the move. A little examination found that a father or mother did the same thing at a similar age or stage in life. It is as if "I have to do this because it is what my family does."

Do you find it difficult to trust? Don't blame yourself. Look at your immediate and historical family. I bet you will find the roots of not trusting in someone's unresolved hurt and pain.

This is not about blaming your past generations for the emptiness in the chambers of your heart. It is not about giving you an excuse for the bad decisions you have made. It is about acknowledging and understanding what happened and how it has affected you. Once you understand the issue, then you have the choice and opportunity to make changes in yourself and for your future generations.

When you are prone to an addiction, fear of intimacy, coldness, or abuse, typically some part of you feels a strong force that is greater than your own issue. I have often explained to my clients that they are carrying the generational problem on their back. Somehow you were chosen or been selected to carry the family burden. Maybe you were chosen because of your sex or place in the birth order. Sometimes we never learn why one is chosen to carry the family pain. I believe it is almost as if there was a family meeting and a vote was taken as to who would be the chosen one to carry the family pain.

Have you been called the "black sheep of the family" or felt like the scapegoat? The family needs you to be this for the family reputation to be continued. While they will say they want you to change, as soon as you try to change, some family member will sabotage it.

There is an interesting history behind the scapegoat concept. In the Bible's Old Testament it is recorded that once a year, at the ceremony of Yom Kippur, the high priest selected a pure, unblemished male goat. He placed his hands on it to symbolize putting all the sins of the people for the full year on the goat, and then drove it into the wilderness. The concept of the scapegoat means that one person bears the blame for all the others. Of course they drive you out of the family or label you as the "black sheep"—because they cannot face their own sin, behavior, and pain. Family members see themselves in you and that is too painful for them to acknowledge. It means they will have to change.

Therefore, whatever you struggle with may not be just your own issue. It may be your father's, grandfather's, or great-grandfather's issue as well. The pain and sin of the past that gets passed on from generation to generation is why the bond is extremely difficult for you to break. You are wrestling with the generational family burden that is from your maternal or paternal side, and possibly both. Though we like to blame mothers for all our pain, the truth is the source is usually equally divided between both sides of the family.

Let me quickly add that you should try not to become discouraged and believe change is impossible. You are not stuck in this dysfunctional family system forever. You can step off this merry-go-round. The fact that you are reading this book indicates that you have a desire to change how you feel, live, and treat your immediate family and friends.

## Breaking The Family Legacy

Today most of us are familiar with O'Hare International Airport in Chicago. It is named after Butch O'Hare, who went to Annapolis and became a Navy pilot during World War II. He became a national hero after many great acts of skill and bravery, including downing five enemy bombers in one night to protect the USS *Lexington* and its crew. Butch became the first Navy pilot to receive the Congressional Medal of Honor.

What most don't know is that his father, Eddie, was a slick, crooked, corrupt lawyer for Al Capone. He had wealth, power, and status. One day, knowing that he would be killed for it, he turned his back on it all, went to the police, and told everything he knew. In spite of his father's known criminal history, Butch applied to Annapolis and was accepted—and he rose above his miserable family history to become a national hero.

If you are experiencing emotional pain that seems much greater than what you have done to yourself, it is very possible that the extra potency is generational. The hole in your heart may be generational and a powerful struggle for you to deal with. Remember, you do have a choice as to whether you wish to live with this pain and pass it on to your children and grandchildren.

*Your Challenge and Opportunity*

Do you want to go to your grave knowing you have passed the generational pain on to your grandchildren? Or do you want to move on, knowing you have given your children and grandchildren more than you received?

You came into this world and immediately became a part of a generational family system that had both the seeds of life and dysfunction in it.

What family legacy are you passing on to your future generations?

# Chapter 11: Rediscovering the Hole in Your Heart

It is inevitable that just when you believe you have overcome a past hurt, something happens that is similar to the original hurt and the old pain is exposed. Or if you deny you have a painful hole in your heart and refuse to work on healing it, you are in for some unpleasant surprises. When you least expect it, the old pain will come rushing back and grab you by surprise.

Both of these situations are similar to one in which you think your old ankle injury is healed — uexpectedly you twist it and let out a cry of pain. You have just discovered that underneath what appeared to be a healed ankle, it was still very tender.

*Some Case Histories*

When Bill's adult son betrayed him, he was devastated. Bill knew he had a history of family rejection and betrayal. He believed his many years of self-exploration and some therapy had helped him deal with his past. For many years, he had lived a very stable life and dealt with other major losses. However, his son's deception really rocked his boat.

It exposed the original hole in his heart, which he believed was reasonably healed.

Sally, a woman in mid-life, was heard saying in regard to her father, "I did not know he could hurt me this much after all these years." When she said this, she had just discovered that her father, who had abandoned her early in life, had done something to hurt her again just before he died.

You have been cruising along quite well in your life feeling confident that you have dealt with or overcome the hole in your heart. Actually, you rarely even think about your early childhood pain. Suddenly your spouse says he or she is leaving you and the stabbing pain, which penetrates the depth of your being, is a combination of the present crisis and the opening of the old wound of abandonment in early life.

Tom had survived a very difficult childhood with abusive alcoholic parents. When he sat in the doctor's office with his wife and heard the doctor say she had cancer, he almost passed out. The day of her surgery, he was so emotionally distraught he could hardly walk. He was so immobilized that the intake person at the hospital thought *he* was the patient. The reality of impending loss was a crisis in the present and a resurrection of an early childhood trauma.

Your mother was verbally abusive. For a number of years in order to control the pain, you greatly limited the amount of time and involvement she had in your life. You did quite well controlling the pain because she was not constantly "at you." Now, you have children and want them to know their grandmother, so you cautiously resume contact. Just as you are beginning to feel guardedly comfortable with her, she verbally attacks you like she did when you were a child. Now both your adult person and the little girl inside you are deeply wounded. You are devastated again. It feels as if the pain is worse than when you were a child.

Or, you think you have overcome the cruel things your mother, father, or sibling said to you as a child. Then you reluctantly go home for Christmas and they do it to you again. The hurt and pain shoots through your body. You want to run away and never go back, but you cannot because you do not want to ruin your children's Christmas. You have just rediscovered the hole in your heart. Rather than dealing with the source of the pain, you vow to never go back. The problem is some other similar circumstance will emerge to reexpose the original pain.

A common resurrection of the pain is for those of you who are adult children of alcoholics. When your spouse or child starts to drink, not necessarily excessively, you begin to panic. You become angry, yell, withdraw, get depressed, or use some other method to attempt to get him to stop. You must find some way to protect yourself from the horrific emotional pain. Your pain is a blending of your early life experiences and what is presently happening to you.

The event may be as innocuous as standing on the street corner waiting for your spouse to pick you up. When your spouse is late, you feel a sense of panic that you quickly convert to anger. When he arrives, no apology or explanation will do, as you are in a full-blown state of anger. This innocuous event has somehow touched an early childhood pain of the terror of being left alone.

When I was eighteen and working in a gas station (in the old days when we actually pumped gas into customers' cars), my boss asked me to run across the street to the VFW tavern and get some change. I thought nothing of it. As I stood at the bar waiting for the change, I came very close to a full-blown panic attack. I quickly grabbed the change and ran out as fast as I could. My early childhood memories of being there with my drunken father caught me completely off guard and overwhelmed me. The hole in my heart had been exposed. As I write this story, I feel some of the emotions, but because I have worked on this, the feelings no longer overwhelm or control me.

One day I was in the midst of doing an executive prehiring assessment on a candidate who was being considered for a major engineering leadership role. I had said, "Sam, you are a very bright, capable person and possibly Mensa." His reaction shocked me. He immediately broke down sobbing from deep in his being and was walking around my office very distraught. I was stunned and wondered, *what did I say to cause this?* After he settled down, I repeated myself because I wanted to be certain I had expressed myself correctly. Again, he immediately went into the same agonizing wail. When he settled down the second time, he said, "No one in my life has ever said that I was bright and competent." I said "You have a bachelor's and master's degrees in engineering and a very successful career." Sam then explained a little bit about his seriously dysfunctional family and his abusive father. He called me a week later to ask if I really meant what I said. I had unknowing hit the hole in his heart that he had so repressed, he did not even know it was there.

If you have the tragic memory of your teenage child being killed in an auto accident while out with friends, your tendency is probably too overprotect your other children so you will not have to endure that horrible pain again. You believe you are protecting your children, but the truth is you are really protecting yourself, because deep in your being you don't believe you could survive the loss of another child. In the counseling profession, there is a truism that states when someone appears to be protecting another person, he is really protecting himself.

*The Gopher Game*

My grandson likes for me to take him to Chuck E. Cheese to play the arcade games. One of his favorites is the gopher game—the little gophers jump out of different holes at unexpected times and the challenge is to see how quickly you can knock them back into the hole with a mallet. Some of you are living lives of desperation. You are trying to repress the unexpected emotions by pushing them back into the subconscious so you don't have to deal with them. The problem is you never know when or where one of these painful memories will pop up. This keeps you in a constant state of anxiety, uptight and alert, prohibiting you from relaxing. Your family, friends, and coworkers are also constantly trying to anticipate when one of these emotions is going to pop up so they do not get clobbered by you.

*How Can We Know?*

How can we know if a present experience has uncovered an old childhood pain?

The litmus test is when your emotional reaction to a current situation is much more intense, painful, and debilitating than you would have expected.

For example: your friend calls at the last minute and cancels an outing the two of you had planned. You become furious and declare you will never speak to her again, and you are in a foul mood the rest the day. Most likely, your old pain of rejection was discovered again.

Here is a way to evaluate if your present emotional pain is only from the present situation or if it is reopening an old wound. Ask yourself:

- Did the degree of the pain seem to be much greater than I would have expected?
- Did I react more strongly to the situation than I would have predicted?
- Did the pain seem to come from deep in my being or was it more a surface reaction?

- Did others around me think I overreacted to the situation?
- Did my behavior result in hurting others?
- Do I seem to frequently react strongly to similar situations?
- Have others ever commented that I need to deal with a past hurt?
- Do I have bouts of depression or anxiety that come after I have had an emotional reaction to a current situation?

The measurement of how well you are doing in overcoming the hole in your heart is twofold. Ask yourself:

- How quickly did I recognize the source of my emotional pain?
- How quickly did I deal with it and restore my equilibrium without repressing the pain?

As you progress in your healing, you will find that you more readily recognize the pain and its source, and are able to bring it under control. Remember, emotional healing is like physical healing. It takes time.

Just when you think you have arrived, God throws you another challenge, giving you the opportunity to grow some more. Remember chapter six (The Joy of Pain)!

# Chapter 12: Growing Beyond

L ife is a journey not an event. Are you going to live to its fullness or be part of the walking dead?

To grow beyond the emptiness, hurt and pain, you must choose to be active in the daily development of your life. It is your life. No one else can develop it for you, and you would not like it or let them if they could.

The real joy of life comes in self-discovery and growing through pain. One of the joys of therapists is watching the depressed or distressed person face himself and find release from his pain. It is amazing to watch the cloud of depression and the pain of life lift and watch the transformation on a patient's face and throughout his body. It is thrilling to see a life change from being a heavy burden to living in joy.

If you need professional assistance to help you work through your hurt and pain, I strongly recommend you seek a therapist who is professionally trained and practices within a family systems model. This means a therapist who will help you look back at your generational family history and learn from the past. He will help you construct a family genogram so you can see your historical family patterns and help you break out of the destructive patterns. He will assist you in developing healthy habits so you can pass them on to your children and grandchildren.

To find a therapist trained in this model visit www.aamft. org.

*The Ten Habits of Emotionally Healthy Living*[23]

1. I will use my pain to become better, not bitter.
2. I will focus daily on finding new ways to becoming an emotionally healthy person.
3. I will immediately forgive each time a painful memory reemerges, or someone offends me.
4. I will give up blaming others.
5. I will be grateful each day for all my blessings, great and small.
6. I will frequently read helpful books and literature.
7. I will encourage and help others who are struggling with their pain.
8. I will keep a daily journal of my journey.
9. I will write my mission in life and review it at least weekly.
10. I will live by the Golden Rule: Do unto others as I wish them to do to me.

I want to challenge you to practice these ten habits each day, and seek to live life to your fullest potential so you will find the joy of life for yourself and your children and your children's children.

# Appendix A: Traits of a Healthy Family

1. A healthy Family communicates and listens.
2. A healthy Family affirms and supports one another.
3. A healthy Family teaches respect for others.
4. A healthy Family developes a sense of trust.
5. A healthy Family has a sense of play.
6. A healthy Family exhibits a sense of shared responsibility.
7. A healthy Family teaches a sense of right and wrong.
8. A healthy Family has a strong sense of gamily in which rituals and traditions abound.
9. A healthy Family has a sense of balance of interaction among members.
10. A healthy Family has a shared religious core.
11. A healthy Family respects the privacy of one another.
12. A healthy Family values service to others.
13. A healthy Family fosters table time and conversation.
14. A healthy Family shares leisure time.
15. A healthy Family admits to and seeks help with problems.

The Traits of a Healthy Family, Delores Curran, Ballantine Books, 1983,

# Appendix B: Children Learn What They Live

If a child lives with criticism. He learns to condemn.

If a child lives with hostility. He learns to fight.

If a child lives with ridicule.He learns to be shy.

If a child lives with shame. He learns to feel guilty.

If a child lives with tolerance. He learns to be patient.

If a child lives with encouragement. He learns confidence.

If a child lives with praise. He learns to appreciate.

If a child lives with fairness. He learns justice.

If a child lives with security. He learns to have faith.

If a child lives with approval. He learns to like himself.

If a child lives with acceptance and friendship. He learns to find love in the world.

(Author Unknown)

# End Notes

## Chapter 1: The Hole in Your Heart

1. Abraham Maslow, *Toward a Psychology of Being* (New York: D. Van Nostrand Company, 1968), 21.
2. Ibid., 22–23.
3. Ibid., 41.

## Chapter 2: Emotionally Dependent

4. Thomas Merton, No Man Is An Island (San Diego: Harcourt Brace Jovanovich, 1955), xv.
5. Rene Spitz, *The First Year of Life* (New York: International Universities Press, 1965), 27–31. The original study was published by Dr. Spitz as "Hospitalism: An Inquiry into the Genesis of Psychiatric Conditions in Early Childhood," in *The Psychoanalytic Study of the Child*, vol. 1 (New Haven: Yale University Press, 1945), and "Hospitalism: A Follow-Up Report," in *The Psychoanalytic Study of the Child*, vol. 2 (1946).

## Chapter 3: No One Can Fulfill Another's Compartment

6. "Baby Drops Introducted in Germany as Infanticide Cases Spike" *Fox News.com*, March 27, 2007.
7. Max Lucado, Facing Your Goliaths (Nashville: Thomas Nelson, 2006), 156–157.

## Chapter 4: The Walking Dead—Are You One of Them?

8. David Keith, Family Therapy As An Alternative to Medication (New York: Brunner-Routledge, 2003), 7–8.
9. Ibid.
10. Goggle, Dr. Aaron T. Beck, Professor of Psychiatry, University of Pennsylvania School of Medicine.

## Chapter 5: Meet Your Monkeys

11. See Appendix A for the article "If A Child Lives With…"
12. Carl Rogers, *On Becoming a Person* (Boston: Houghton Mifflin Company, 1961), 33–35.

## Chapter 7: The Joy of Pain

13. Leo Tolstoy, Anna Karenin (Russia: Ruskil Vestnik, 1877), 1.
14. C. S. Lewis, The Problem of Pain, (Glasgow: William Collins Sons & Company, 1961), 84.
15. Ibid., 81.
16. Ibid., 95.
17. Victor Frankel, *The Unconscious God* (New York: Simon & Shuster, 1975), 137.

## Chapter 8: Bitter or Better

18. Rollo May, The Art of Counseling (Nashville: Abingdon Press, 1967), 35.
19. Abraham Maslow, *Toward a Psychology of Being* (New York: D. Van Nostrand Company, 1968), 46.

## Chapter 9: Healing the Hole in Your Heart

20. P. W. Coleman, "The Process of Forgiveness in Marriage and the Family," *Exploring Forgiveness*, ed. R. D. Enright and J. North (Madison, WI: The University of Wisconsin Press, 1998), 78.
21. Merriam-Webster Collegiate Dictionary, Version 2.5 (Springfield: Merriam-Webster, 2000).

## Chapter 12: Growing Beyond

22. The word habits used in this context has been popularized by Steven Covey. I did an extensive search to find a different and more suitable word but could not find one. Rather than use a second-best word, I want to give appreciation to Mr. Covey for bringing this word to the forefront in his writings. A habit is a behavior pattern acquired by frequent repetition or an acquired behavior that has become nearly or completely involuntary.

Printed in the United States
102808LV00002B/139-237/P